How to Be a Great Husband

How to Be
a Great
Husband

by Tobias Jungreis

Vital Issues Press

Vital Issues Press
P.O. Box 53788
Lafayette, Louisiana 70505

Cover photo copyright © 1996,
Comstock, Inc.

Library of Congress Card Catalog
Number 96-060582
ISBN 1-56384-120-7

Printed in the U.S.A.

Dedication

This book is dedicated to my wife, Shirley, the object of my intense love. She is a selfless "giving tree" to all those fortunate enough to have personally or professionally come into contact with her.

This book is dedicated, as well, to my children who grew up with a father who was a husband first and a father second. Yet, these same children blossomed into absolutely wonderful, quality human beings.

And lastly, this book is dedicated to my ever-missed parents, whose close, loving, though tempestuous, relationship laid the framework for those aspects of my marriage that were to be savored and enhanced, lived up to and perpetuated.

Contents

Live happily with the woman you love through the fleeting days of life, for the wife God gives you is your best reward down here for all your earthly toil.

—Ecclesiastes 9:9

Preface

I have been blessed with a special wife, many extremely happy years of marriage, and four wonderful children. I also have been blessed with the ability to love intensely and with energy and imagination.

It is in gratitude for these multiple blessings that I have written this book. I wanted to share my joy and experience; to encourage closer, friendlier marriages; to encourage husbands to expend the energy that is necessary to keep a union joyful and strong; to challenge couples to reach for the greatest heights of marital achievement; to push women to shoot for the moon and demand the best from their men. I pray that as a result of these efforts, others will be blessed as I have been.

Introduction

Why would a young man entering marriage set as his lifetime goal—his highest priority, his ultimate dream—to be the best husband ever? It's a bit unusual, to say the least. Most males approaching adulthood have more traditional, though certainly very acceptable, goals in life: to be a millionaire by age thirty, to cure cancer, to be a TV star or a computer wizard, to marry Cybill Shepherd, to be president of the United States, to invent something incredible, to walk on the moon—even to be the best father. But, to want to be the best husband?

To some, this goal sounds wimpy. It is an achievement never bragged about, and if it is, the bragging is often meant to draw attention to some other accomplishment or evidence of power or wealth (for example, the guy who gives his wife an expensive diamond bracelet as a reminder to all that he just became CEO of a Fortune 500 corporation). It is certainly not table talk amongst ordinary people, as would be the dream of hitting a hole in one, or bowling a perfect game, or making a killing in the stock market.

Success as a husband usually is not a visible achievement, at least publicly, unless you count smiling faces and apparently contented individuals. Often a great husband has problems with his contemporaries *because* of his devotion to his wife. He's less available for bowling with the guys at night. In fact, he's less free in general and rarely acts spontaneously without his wife's input. His devotion sometimes embarrasses less caring husbands when he and his wife are out with other couples. In summary, he's often less than a great friend because, by choice, *his* best friend—sometimes his *only* close friend—is his wife.

What possible motivations energize an individual to set out to be an extraordinary husband? Is it to compensate for an unhappy childhood, or perhaps a home of origin filled with yelling and tension (or even wife abuse)? Is it that some men are born to serve and please another person to an extreme degree? Is it the wife herself who creates her husband's need to treasure her because *she* is needy or desperate for love, or because her appreciation strikes some chord in her mate and drives him into even greater degrees of nurturing? Is it that some males cannot get as much satisfaction from their work or other relationships to compare with the validation they get from taking care of their wives? Or, is it simply just chemistry, whereby a man is so taken, so smitten with his bride, that he is driven to want to please her?

The truth of the matter is that a man's motivation doesn't matter. If a man can work hard at being an expert husband, he will reap very generous rewards. A woman who receives the caring and devotion and attention and unconditional love and time and support and entertainment and loyalty of her husband (whew!) will reward her hard-working husband for his efforts every minute of his life. A woman who is loved will return the love she receives to her mate in geometric proportions.

It is especially vital today to restore understanding, communication, and closeness between marital partners. The divorce rate in this country is catastrophically high and numerous alternative lifestyles have emerged. Clearly, the sacred institution of marriage has lost its firm footing, with the result that fewer and fewer children are receiving the secure foundation that comes from growing up in a stable, loving, two-parent home.

If we are to restore our society to health, we must first strengthen its basic building block—the family unit. In order to flourish, this unit must be anchored by a contented, giving wife who is, in turn, nourished by the love of a supportive and faithful husband. God must come first in both of their lives, but their faith is the only thing that should be more important to either of them than the needs of the other.

It takes effort to keep a marriage strong and dynamic and *fun*. But, husbands willing to make that effort will be blessed with the greatest treasure on earth: a happy marriage that lasts a lifetime.

Chapter One

The Premise:
Till Death Do Us Part

If, indeed, a husband and his wife are going to spend their whole lives working on becoming best friends and achieving true unity of the soul and the heart, then they must function on the premise that they have a marriage contract that is a lifetime one; that this contract is etched in stone; and that the contract will remain in effect until the death of one of its members. Committing to this premise actually makes it easier for the partners. There is no way out; therefore, it must succeed. However, it will only succeed if it is constantly worked on, improved, honored, respected, refreshed, savored, and enjoyed. It must be fully understood. The obligations of each of the mates to one another have to be clarified.

The premise "till death do us part" means that the man and woman who fell in love with each other are willing to undertake the nonstop effort that is required to make this relationship succeed. Now, this is a pretty tall order for most people to comprehend. Whether they admit it or not, most of their commitment is based on their being physically attracted to each other, their enjoyment of each other's personality, and the fact that they are loved by the other. Often, two youngsters have a whirlwind courtship of only a month or two before they rush off to get married. When you think of it, they are agreeing to a fifty- or sixty-year contract based on little more than a state of mind and a hope. That's scary.

In addition to their current blissful state of mind and attraction, our two perpetrators are making this long-range commitment on the basis of other factors as well, many of which are flimsy and without foundation. Keep in mind the fact that when they first meet one another, they are carrying the "baggage" and ideas from their tender upbringings. One of the partners might be marrying to get out of an unhappy home situation. One might be marrying because only the young married executives in the office are considered for advancement. One might be fearful that he or she is getting older and all the best potential mates are already taken. She might be accepting his proposal because she wants to have children and is fearful of her biological clock running out.

So, in summary, these two people, blinded by infatuation and shaped by a lifetime of different experiences, declare their love to each other and run off gleefully to find a diamond ring and a catering hall. How is it possible that they can even begin to absorb what they are getting into?

And, what preparations are required of them before they sign up for this lifelong commitment? Some states require a blood test. All states require a marriage license. Individuals with certain religious affiliations must follow the required laws and procedures of their faith. There is a minimum age requirement. That's it! Most newlyweds will have to struggle with their new relationship and learn whatever they can "on the job."

Some religious organizations address this problem by having local counsellors come speak to groups of singles and young married couples, but most don't have this kind of forum in place. It might be helpful if school hygiene classes focused less on health and body mechanics and more on understanding people and their natures. It would certainly seem worthwhile to offer a course or two on "Healthy Ideas to Make Marriages Joyous and Fulfilling" or "How to Be a Friend in Marriage." Perhaps, if this were done, there would be less demand for adult education courses on "Single Parenting" and "Equitable Distribution."

But, back to our couple and the contract fixed in stone. What happens if problems arise? The two of them are arguing. They're not talking. They need help. From the minute they say "I do," they know that they are obligated to repair the hurts and misunderstandings that are normal for any relationship. Unlike a casual friendship, they cannot walk out or sweep their difficulties under a rug, nor can they practice denial. They have to face up to the rough spots and deal with them. This marriage contract is serious and binding. It requires constant honing, refining, and

clarification. The ecstatic glee of courtship and engagement should gradually
give way to a more solid, realistic, and
mature enjoyment of one another.

If the couple cannot correct the difficulties by themselves, they should run—
not walk—to get professional help. And,
they should do it early in marriage, before deep rifts set in, before they hurt
each other, and before permanent scars
become deeply entrenched. Hopefully,
they can get back on track and restore
their trust and dependency on each other.

Their mentality must be that they have
to succeed. They must be prepared to sac-
rifice whatever it takes to make their relationship work and sparkle. There is no
alternative choice. The laughing optimism
that they had, skipping hand-in-hand
when they first met, propelled them into
legalizing their union. If their awareness
and sensitivity mature at the same rate as
their years do, and if their ability to focus
and act responsibly grows as well, then
the gamble of these two people, based on
hope and a dream, will return them rich
dividends.

Scripture tells us that "love covereth
all sins" (Prov. 10:12). If a man fills his
wife's life with unconditional devotion and

caring, she will give him, in return, enormous amounts of love, respect, and loyalty—and vice versa. Love *is* a many splendored thing.

Chapter Two

Men and Women Are Delightfully Different

Women might be very different from men, but God created them wonderfully! They are physically soft and graceful. They are gentle beings. When a male and female driver inadvertently converge on the same parking spot, it is usually the woman who will back off first and give the man the parking space. Whether driving on the road, standing in a supermarket line, going in and out of a door, or dealing with most confrontational or competitive situations in life, it is typically the woman, in her soft way, who will let the more urgent man go first.

In fact, men and women approach life differently in almost every respect. Men like to talk about how much money they are making or saving or investing. Every man knows where to buy some item cheap in order to make his buddies jealous. Guys share their winning stock market victories. (Losses? Who has losses?) Guys know where in Hong Kong to have great dress shirts made for pennies. They know how to get money from the insurance company after a loss and turn it into a profit; they know how to wrap up all their assets in convoluted trusts. Money, for guys, is not just for acquiring, or for putting to a good use, or for upgrading one's life. For many men, the pursuit of money is an invigorating challenge and an endless game. It is a constant subject of conversation in a gathering of males.

Sports talk is another constant in most male gatherings. As one athletic season comes to a close with its rounds of play-offs and finals, another is always beginning. One athlete or another is always doing something that borders on the unbelievable. Some star is always getting arrested, or is in a brawl or a salary dispute, or is being traded, or is letting us down in the clutch. Sports fans have fierce loyalties and rivalries, and guys never tire of discussing them.

Women, on the other hand, talk about relationships and feelings. Their ups and downs are triggered by the slightest nuances in a conversation with a relative or a friend, a neighbor or a co-worker. Little things do mean a lot to them—a gift, a personal note, a tone of voice, an invitation, a compliment, a run in a stocking, the height of a heel, a new set of earrings, burnt cookies, running into an old flame, a baby's smile . . . The small occurrences of everyday life often have a great impact on a woman.

More than for a man, a woman's state of mind centers around her feelings and moods, which in turn are sometimes affected by her hormonal cycle. (Men also swing hormonally, though to a lesser extent, although few will admit it.) Thus, a married woman has as her partner a man who is created to be very different from her and who functions on a totally different wavelength.

Even if a man has grown up in a house full of sisters, he may find understanding his wife to be a challenge. He thinks of himself as rational, organized, and predictable; therefore, he's perplexed when his wife is emotional for no apparent reason, unaffectionate when, by every reason, she ought not to be, illogical in the face of contradictory evidence, and sometimes just sad when everything is going wonderfully.

Her mysterious behavior will not respond to the usual problem solving to which he is accustomed. When she is unhappy, he often cannot reason her out of it, rush her out of it, bribe her out of it, distract her out of it, or bulldoze her out of it.

The same man who breezily supervises ten employees during his workday, keeps a crisp schedule of appointments, wins over his toughest customers, fits in an hour of squash, and is considered one of the best young executives in the industry, sometimes comes home and finds himself absolutely inept when he attempts to figure out, or even communicate with, his wife.

A man's world centers around success in the workplace, accumulating material goods, achieving social status, being popular with his buddies, staying in the best physical shape, and becoming a responsible community citizen. A woman's life, on the other hand, revolves around her relationships, her kids, her home, her nurturing instincts, and her feelings and emotions. Understanding and accepting these differences are crucial. They are an integral part of God's grand design.

Instead of becoming impatient with his wife's greater sensitivity, a wise husband recognizes its value. After all, it's this very sensitivity that enables his wife to anticipate and fulfill so many of his own needs so well.

Chapter Three

A Good Marriage
Needs Lots of Work

They tell the story of the government inspector who slapped a stiff fine on a butcher, charging him with false advertising. Said the inspector, "You advertise that you are selling rabbit burgers, but our laboratory found that the burgers are almost all horse meat, rather than the 50 percent rabbit meat that the law requires for such advertising." "But," protested the butcher, "they *are* 50 percent rabbit and 50 percent horse. One rabbit and one horse!"

To say that a husband and wife labor equally during their marriage, teaching the other what each knows best, working out their differences, and sharing the workload of their family, to me, would be inaccurate and oversimplifying—another "rabbit burger" story.

It is true that some husbands show their wives the basics of routine car maintenance, such as how to check the oil or the air in the tires, if their wives don't already know how. Other husbands teach their mates to play tennis or golf, or how to fish. Still others show their wives simple electrical or plumbing repair tricks they've learned along the way.

Most women, on the other hand, don't just teach their husbands the things that they know how to do better, such as sewing on a button or baking a cake or covering the kids' schoolbooks. Wives do much more. They spend every day of their married lives teaching their mates to be better people. They take this raw, masculine male, steeped in rules and manly energy, and slowly go through the process of making him a more gentle human being. Proverbs clearly acknowledges this valuable trait in a wife: "She openeth her mouth with wisdom; and in her tongue is the law of kindness" (Prov. 31:26).

A woman's lifetime work on her man is awesome. It is exhausting—mentally, physically, and emotionally. It is constant (yes, daily). It is not something for which she gets thanked; instead, her efforts are often resisted and resented. Her work never ends because the victories achieved in one decade often don't apply to the new situations that life brings on in the following decade.

Some wives are more skilled at this necessary instruction than others. Some just cannot do it. (Who says you don't marry a man to change him? What planet are they living on?) Some women hide this process better than others. The successful ones rarely show their work publicly but rather work with little whispers in his ear or gentle coaxing behind closed doors.

The less fortunate ones will be chiding their guys with others around, often so frustrated that dignity or vanity or image are totally irrelevant. The woman who fails completely is an outwardly angry or inwardly depressed individual. She who manages half the job alternates between a happy and a sad person, joyous when he is loving and responding appropriately but in despair when he is stubborn or just thick. The successful lady enjoys the fruits of her work (if she's not too exhausted by the time she gets to that point) and can, for the most part, enjoy having a partner who understands and adores her.

If a man is aware that he is getting this free training program, he will, if he is wise, sit back and enjoy it. He will learn how to listen. He'll learn how to communicate clearly and inoffensively. He'll learn how to express appreciation and love. In fact, he'll learn how to skillfully declare all his feelings and emotions. He will clearly state that he is afraid of failure or is feeling disappointed or sexually needy or frightened or jealous or inadequate or inferior or in pain or embarrassed, rather than just lumping them under "being angry." He will also explain that he feels pride or satisfaction or closeness or relief or reassurance or appreciation or good fortune or validation or manliness or warmth, as opposed to "I'm feeling good" or "I'm happy."

Depending on how long he's been married (and how far along he is in his ongoing training program), a husband is a mix of his original raw state, with the "baggage" he brings into the marriage, and the seemingly endless modifications and improvements his wife has imposed on him or negotiated with him. Some of the changes a husband makes will be effectuated by a single explanatory conversation, while other changes will take his wife's persistent, exhausting efforts over many years.

In a successful marriage, both mates must work hard at changing the habits and behaviors that irritate the other. However, it is usually the husband who will need to change the most. Keep in mind that a woman is sometimes deeply affected by things that a man might not even notice. So, if squeezing the toothpaste in the middle or leaving your socks on the living room floor sets your wife's teeth on edge, don't do it! Honoring her simple requests will show her that her happiness, even in little things, matters to you.

If you strive to understand the different emotional needs of your wife, your efforts will be amply rewarded. Your relationship will be drastically improved, and you will find your home blessed with true harmony, a welcome refuge from the stresses of your job and the outside world.

Chapter Four

Communication between Husband and Wife

It gives a woman great pleasure to know that her husband thinks about her constantly. And, if he does indeed think of her throughout his day, he should make sure that she knows it.

Too often, a man who bears great love for his wife will make it difficult for her to know the depth of his feeling. Many men grow up in households where emotion, positive or negative, is rarely expressed. They never learned to say "I love you" or "I'm very appreciative," and often they have never stated verbally "I resent you" or "I'm dreadfully disappointed." In some cases, their role models—their fathers—never talked about feelings very much. In other cases, they were literally taught that men, *real* men, are "strong." They are above feelings, and when they are "weak" enough to sense an emotion stirring from within, they take pride in never letting it show. Men aren't supposed to cry or have a tear in their eyes. It's "sissyish." It's unmanly.

So, what happens when a male who functions skillfully during his workday by never letting crises "get to him," who keeps a cool calm when the tension rises, who earns the most points by maintaining his impassive profit motive amongst his co-workers, suddenly returns to his home at 7:00 P.M.? When he walks in the door, the rules suddenly change. He has to shift gears. He must greet his wife with a kiss, tell her he missed her and that he loves her, and ask her how her day was.

I have listened to wives describe their mates. "He's not much of a talker, but I can tell, from the little hints I get, when he's happy or discontented, or when he's feeling good about me or brooding over something." This sounds like something out of a poem about Paul Revere: "One if by land, two if by sea." If he has such and such a look on his face, it means "this." If he grunts twice, it means "that." If he suddenly leaves the room during a discussion, it means that he has decided that the conversation is over! (And, if he slams the door, she knows that he's mad and that she's right in the argument!)

A husband should openly express his feelings for his wife instead of leaving her to guess what they are. He should compliment her and give her positive reinforcement for all that she does. He should tell her she is beautiful and that he loves her every day of his life. A woman thrives on a steady diet of loving words. Specifically, he should tell her that he adores her every day, and that he finds her incredibly gorgeous.

For example, he might tell her that her hair is glistening with highlights, is deliciously soft, or smells great. (This is a particularly wonderful compliment to give a woman when she's about to leave for a social occasion where it's important to her to look right and feel right.) He might remind her what a great figure she has or that her eyes are dazzling. A husband must tell his wife daily that she is the most important thing in his life—more than his work, more than the children, more than his stocks, and even (are you ready?) more . . . more important than his mother!

Competing Roles

Almost every man is both a husband and a father. Balancing these two roles is sensitive and certainly not casual. Of course, ideally, he should be a wonderful dad to his kids and the perfect mate to his wife. However, time constraints and energy limitations often put these two roles in conflict, with the result that he has the uncomfortable task of choosing his priorities. A working man who returns home at 7:00 P.M. and drops off to sleep at midnight has to apportion those five hours in between to homework with the kids, gazing into his wife's eyes, having supper with his family, some phone calls, a hot bath, and possibly finishing some work brought home from the office. (This assumes no TV!) With his energy draining, how long does he have for each activity, and in what order?

It is my firm opinion that the time spent with his wife in the evening should be his highest priority, though granted, the other items are very important. He should ask her how her day was—with whom did she speak? is there anything new to take care of? what are her worries? her disappointments? her version of how the kids are doing? If he is interested and is an attentive listener, the marriage will be a firm one. And, more likely than not, if the marriage is firm, his wife, who is also the mother of his children, will bring up a great set of kids for him, well adjusted and well loved. (And, hopefully, in our example of five short hours, he will also find the time to hug his kids, listen to them, inquire into their day, and maybe even quiz them for their upcoming tests.)

The husband who contracted to love, honor, and obey his precious mate until "death do us part" should check in with the object of this contract as soon as he enters his busy home—before looking through the mail, checking to see what's for supper, getting something to drink, or turning on the TV. He is probably unaware of how much she desperately needs his interest and concern, how much she leans on him for emotional strength, and how everything once again will be all right once she has unburdened herself and perceives that she has his support. (The odds are very good that when he in turn unburdens the experiences of his day, his contented and very loved wife will be a

reliable source of strength for him also, if
he has the skills to share events and feelings in a complete and honest manner,
which, as we have observed, is not something to be taken for granted.)

To summarize, our husband (under
voluntary contract) will express his love
for his wife every day with words of his
own that are audible and show her by his
behavior that he really means it. In order
to demonstrate the appropriate behavior,
he must study her, listen to her, get to
know her needs and expectations, get to
know what delights her and excites her,
and get to know her yearnings and dreams
and deep pain. What hurtful "history" has
she brought to this marriage that has to
be discussed and dealt with and set free?
What relationships in her life are disap-
pointing and haunting? What means of
self-expression would make her a complete person? What untold stories of her
childhood is she yearning to share? What
are her hopes and expectations for your
children? What vacations does she dream
of? What kind of a house does she fanta-
size over that would transform her into
the mistress of a magical castle? What skills
would she be thrilled to acquire?

There is so much to learn about her. How does she feel about you? Are you the soul mate that she counted on? Her prince charming? Are you romantic enough? Are you the role model for the kids that she feels so strongly that her husband ought to be? Does she like your eating habits? Your hair style? Your posture? Your clothing? Your neckties? Is she proud of you when she's with her relatives? Are you supportive enough of her friends? Is she insecure over money because you're not demonstrating responsibility or diligence in your work?

Or, conversely, is she sad that you're a slave to your business and that she cannot see enough of you? Does she have to share personal problems with friends or relatives because she doesn't have your time (or your ear)?

The cute schoolgirl or polished young woman who attracted your eye, dallied you through a bouncy courtship, mesmerized you into thinking that you were the one who was proposing—this girl is to become the primary focus of your life? You have to actually *study* her—like going to school again. This is work! Why didn't someone warn you, or at least prepare you? Everyone else just seemed to fall into marriage effortlessly. When you see other couples, they are laughing and snuggling together; they seem to be natural pals. But, don't you believe it. Remember that half of all marriages end in divorce, and of the remaining half that stay together, it is absolutely impossible to know how they're getting along, how close they really are. Frequently, when a couple splits up, their best friends are shocked, their relatives are in disbelief, and even their children never dreamt that things were that bad.

But, fear not. You are a romantic. You are a communicator. You have the right attitude. You pray daily. You are prepared to make the effort. You have put your faith in God. You will have a wondrous, fulfilling marriage.

Chapter Five

Active Listening

A husband will succeed in solidifying his marriage if he learns the skill of listening to his wife and responding appropriately. He must hear her message—act on it, learn from it, and respond to it. The art of listening, *real* listening, is a rarity but is not a lost art. It never was! People are often just too wrapped up in their own lives, too impatient, and too easily distracted to focus on and absorb what a speaker is saying. How many people do we know that we can count on to actually sit through our description of a personal problem or a trip we recently took?

How many will listen attentively to our feelings about a film or a book?

Active listening is a term used for genuine listening in which the listener receives from the speaker's message the emotional impact and the true feelings voiced. These go far beyond the "literal" content and the words actually used.

Active listening is a difficult skill. A husband arriving home from his office takes one step in the front door, sniffs the aroma coming from the kitchen, and yells to his wife, "Are we having meat loaf again tonight?" His words seem to be a complaint about a boring upcoming meal. His *real* message would elicit from his wife (who is hopefully an accomplished active listener), "Honey, you've really had a hard day." She has heard that he has arrived home worn-out and irritable from a frustrating day, not that he's unhappy over the number of times she prepares meat loaf each month.

Whose Story Is It?

We all have different friends. There is something in particular that we have in common with each of them. We don't necessarily have to like everything about these individuals, but we do have some things in common with them. We may have "activity" friends who like to do one or more things that we also like to do, such as sailing, antiquing, going to the opera, or playing racquetball—all of which we enjoy immensely. However, we might find these very same people terribly boring if we had to sit across from them in a restaurant for an hour and a half.

Similarly, a young mother might share hours with another young mother while their toddlers play together at a preschool group. But, once the babies are out of the picture, these same women, without that one area in common, might totally dislike each other on the basis of different lifestyles and values. Likewise, there are friends whom we never really get to know but who are so adventurous that they make perfect traveling companions.

The rarest type of friends are the "listening" friends. These are people who have enough inner peace to be able to set aside their own agenda and experiences long enough to absorb what you have to say without it setting off so many inner reactions that you, the speaker, are lost from the picture. They are genuinely interested in *you*.

Don't get me wrong. As we listen to someone talking, it is perfectly natural to internalize or personalize that which we are hearing because it reminds us of a similar experience we had, especially if our experience was accompanied by a strongly positive or negative reaction. But, this personalization is so constant or so strong in some of our acquaintances, either because their needs are so great or because they have an enormous array of emotions constantly churning away within them, that they cannot begin to realize that the story being told is not theirs. They forget that someone else is speaking.

When dealing with a person who is too preoccupied to listen, we often slip out of the speaking mode and into the comfortable role of listener (because the one who cannot listen usually has a lot to say). This is perfectly fine. It avoids frustration, and we save our words for someone who, experience has shown, is really interested in them.

We've all experienced this in a social setting when we attempted to tell a story that had an impact on us that same day. We start, "I took my son, Victor, to Dr. Schnall today because he was running a high fever for three days. When I got to his office—" At this point you've gotten out one and a half sentences. (Don't be unhappy. That's well above average!) The listening group, who has absolutely no idea of why this story was so upsetting to you, leaps into action, like color commentators on a football broadcast.

"You know, the flu has been going around the whole neighborhood."

"My son, David, also had a fever last week."

"Oh, I wouldn't use Dr. Schnall. He disappointed me once too often."

"How come you waited three days before you took him?"

"How is Victor doing with his piano lessons?"

"You know I had a similar experience yesterday. It must be a full moon."

"Do you think the global warming is affecting our health?"

"I think the principal should have a policy about sick kids coming to school."

"I saw Mrs. Schnall on the avenue just last week getting into her new Jag."

"Boy, I wouldn't buy a German car."

"I don't think people are having enough roughage these days."

"Victor forgot to return my son's sled."

"I think doctors overcharge these days."

"I would never let my son be a doctor."

"You have to go out of the neighbor-hood to get a good pediatrician."

"Thank God, there are a few good gynecologists."

Etc., etc., etc.! It's really "me, me, me, me" and "my, my, my, my" and "I, I, I, I." Forget it! But, if you are determined to blast your way through the onslaught of nonstop interruptions from this self-centered gaggle of nonlisteners (through the sheer forcefulness of your personality and the increasing volume of your story telling voice), be prepared for the sympathetic and empathetic responses that await you when you finish your tale of woe (which consumed a whole five minutes).

Your six-year-old son had put a cherry pit up his nose. He told no one, was in pain, ran a fever, and stopped eating. You went to Dr. Schnall, who referred you to the eye, ear, nose, and throat man, who referred you to the radiologist, who referred you to the surgeon, who put off the possible surgery for as long as it would take to get the fever down. Sure enough, Victor got off the couch today, tripped over the Yellow Pages phone book, banged his head on the edge of the rattan table, and the pit was jarred out of his nose. It fell on the floor, and you were able to relax for the first time in four days. Ready?

"That reminds me, they never delivered my Yellow Pages this spring."

"I heard Waldbaum's is having a sale on cherries this week."

"You can get good rattan furniture in Hong Kong."

"If my son insisted on being a doctor, I certainly wouldn't let him become a radiologist . . ."

What is so sad is that the teller of this painful story never got what she was after when she shared the sequence of events. She never got the feeling that they were really listening, that the group stepped back from their own agendas long enough to absorb their friend's horrible experience. They never validated her feeling of great concern. In the terminology of active listening, they never reflected back to the speaker the emotional feelings that lay behind the actual facts of the episode. They never gave her the satisfaction that they indeed absorbed what she went through.

In marriage, you must learn how to listen proficiently if you want to make your lady happy and keep your relationship a solid one. You must become an expert "listening friend." A woman who cannot get you to hear her messages will be angry, resentful, and frustrated, and this will immediately reflect itself in her behavior to you, which will in turn set the tone of your day-to-day living. On the positive side, if your wife can share with you her sadnesses, her joys, and her longings, you have become her soul mate, and you'll be one of the lucky ones who is blessed with a great marriage.

Chapter Six

Intimacy

For reasons of delicacy, this chapter was intentionally kept abbreviated. It is expected that two people who care for each other will do just fine and can work out the ifs, ands, and buts of this aspect of marriage. However, since boys will be boys, it's hard to resist a few suggestions.

Be sure that your wife is pleased before you are. For the most part, men crumple into mush after they are pleased, and this makes it more difficult for them to summon up the extreme patience and slow gentleness that are needed to please their lady. In addition, except for those times when both of you are filled with spontaneous, uncontrollable, heated passion, it is best to plan beforehand. Carefully arrange the time and place of those intimate trysts. Otherwise, unpredictable children, too-close-for-comfort houseguests, noisy springs, forgotten paraphernalia, or a wailing cat can spoil all the fun.

Conversely, if you're going to be married for fifty or more years (forget the current statistics, guys; you have given your word), keep the intimate experience fresh with periodic variations. Keep thinking and working, as in other aspects of the marriage, and don't worry—you'll come up with something. Outdoors can be wonderful compared to indoors, the location being limited only by your imagination. There are different times of the day, and furniture other than Sealy Posturpedic. Just be very sure that the lady-in-waiting shares and approves of your well-meaning spirit of adventure.

Very early in the marriage, it is imperative that both partners express any dissatisfaction regarding any aspect of their loving moments. This is extremely difficult for newlyweds (especially for those who were fortunate enough to have withheld physical intimacy until after the wedding ceremony). The admission of being less than satisfied requires great courage. The naming of different locations of the body and having to say them out loud is awfully awkward for two beginners. But, this large area of a working relationship must be addressed. There is an enormous difference between men and women in this area—the timing, the setting, the physiology, the romantic prerequisites, the urgency, what it all represents, the "after play," the frequency, the amount of talking, the lighting—a guy's perspective is so different from that of his wife. He would never dream what goes through her head, and she would never dream what *doesn't* go through his.

As is well known, a woman needs deep emotional closeness to her man before she can be intimate with him, while a man more often feels that deep emotional closeness after he is intimate with his woman. With such a major difference between the sexes, it shouldn't be surprising that problems sometimes surface.

Husbands, the onus is on you to make things right in this area. You must initiate the educational discussions that will help you iron out your differences. You can tell her what your needs are. (That's usually the easy part.) But, getting her to talk requires loving tenderness so she can trust you and be brave enough to describe heretofore unmentionable sensitive details. The rewards, however, are wondrous. A physically pleased woman has a profound contentment. She knows that her man has to love her very much to arrive at the point where he knows how to please her, and he has to work hard and thoroughly to learn how to reach this point.

Since feeling loved and adored is at least as critical to a woman as the physical aspects of these intimate times are, it wouldn't hurt to smother her, before and after the physical moments, with compliments and loving words. Tell her how lovely she looks, how much of a temptress she is, and how young she acts. Observe her various features and remark on how special they are (just never compare her, no matter how favorably, to a girlfriend from your past). Hug her just for the sake of hugging. A women wants to be young, to be beautiful, to be desirable. She wants to know that her husband still yearns for her. An increasingly aware husband will become more skillful at saying the words that fulfill these longings. The ultimate goal is the right blend of love, warmth, respect, closeness (both physical and non-physical), tenderness, gentleness, romance, and friendship—a goal well worth the lifetime of work that it takes to achieve.

And lastly, never lose sight of what this very special aspect of marriage entails. In the words of the Almighty, keep it sacred.

Chapter Seven

Little Things That Make a Big Difference

Protect Her Strength

Besides honoring and loving your bride, it is incumbent on you to protect her physical strength. Her wonderful, attractive body has to bring up the children (if you're so blessed), run the household, do the cooking and the laundry, do spring cleaning, make beds for visiting relatives (including yours), buy and deliver gifts, attend funerals if you can't be there, possibly fit in her own job, and be available to spend time with you, looking rested and appealing.

In reality, most women are physically smaller than their mates. When they are younger, they are often encumbered by pregnancy and by childbirth, and when older, their graceful, feminine bones gradually suffer calcium loss. They are sometimes hampered in different degrees by menstrual and hormonal discomforts. There are many things a caring husband can do, however, to help his wife conserve her strength.

Do the heavy food shopping for her, like getting the frozen turkeys and the cartons of canned sodas. If she shops, bring the bags in from the car to the kitchen. Move heavy cartons or furniture for her. If you know her routine, you're able to anticipate her needs before she has to ask for help. Lift the kids, wash the dishes, carry the suitcases, and move the dresser when something has fallen behind it and needs to be retrieved. If she's in bed ready to sleep and you're still doing paperwork, don't let her get up if she needs something like a drink or two aspirins. Go downstairs and get them for her. Open the heavy door for her, make your own bed, and carry the heavy laundry bag.

If your wife also holds down a job, even a part-time one, make sure you're doing your share of the housework. Studies and polls continue to show that working women still perform the majority of the chores around the house. Consider hiring someone to come in and do the major cleaning on a regular basis. This will do more to make your wife's life easier than you can imagine, and it doesn't require a great deal of money. High-school and college students routinely advertise for housekeeping work, and most of them charge very reasonable rates.

Think of what you can do without in order to fit this extra household help into your budget. Is that weekly magazine subscription really crucial to your health and well-being? Does your office have a microwave? By eating lunch in, you probably can save enough to pay someone to help with the housework at least twice a month.

All of the above is really obvious and straightforward, of course. Once you and your wife have worked hard on your close friendship and you're both really "in sync" and adept at communicating with one another, there is a higher level of assistance that you can provide for her, one that goes far beyond lifting heavy objects or making sure she has the help she needs around the house. If she is sensitive to temperature changes of the tiniest degree that you yourself never experience (my wife gets a chill if I open the ashtray in the car!), be aware of this need. If you're heading out for a drive and the weather is supposed to change, remind her to take an umbrella or a sweater. Yes, it's her need, and you are reminding her. That's what soul mates are for. Let's face it. If you're both going someplace and she's uncomfortable because she's cold, her discomfort will make you uncomfortable, and your whole outing will be negatively affected.

So, before you leave the house, ask yourself what outer clothing you will need and automatically oversee what she's wearing. She might be distracted enough by other matters to overlook something as obvious as a sweater or coat.

There are many ways you can anticipate your wife's needs. If she has a habit of skipping breakfast and finding herself famished before lunch, keep this in mind when you plan for trips. Bring something for her to drink or snack on or schedule a mid-morning break for coffee or brunch. If you know she has a particularly hectic week ahead, offer to pitch in and do whatever would help her out the most.

A husband's job is to physically and emotionally take good care of his wife. If he can accomplish this, then she can in turn more easily take care of the many obligations she has by virtue of the inner and outer strength with which he has provided her.

The Important Phone Calls

Before heading home, whether you're leaving the office, the health club, or anywhere else, phone your wife and ask her if she needs for you to pick up anything for her. Though she might be in charge of food shopping for the house, there are always a couple of miscellaneous items that slip through even the most foolproof checklist: an ingredient for a cake she decides to bake when surprise guests call to say they're dropping by, a battery, toilet paper, diapers, a lime. All are routine items until the last one suddenly runs out. Your wife could get them herself, but maybe she ran out of time or ran out of strength. Maybe she's watching the baby, or a roast is in the oven, or she's covering schoolbooks, or she's not dressed, or you have the car. Phone her! Ask, "What can I bring you that would put a smile on your face or make your nonstop day of running the house just one iota easier?"

Your wife will adore this call. Even if she needs nothing, she'll be thrilled to think that her husband, driving home after a whirlwind day of his own, is thinking of what would please her.

The second very important phone call you owe your lady is the call you make from the supermarket just before you get to the checkout line to buy the items on the shopping list that she gave you. (It has come to my attention that there are men who refuse to do food shopping or avoid it like the plague. Is it a sign of weakness to be seen with a shopping cart or beneath one's dignity? The simple fact is that certain items, such as juices, frozen turkey, and soda, are very heavy when bagged, and your carrying them for her is no less a romantic act than the courtesy of opening a door for her or assisting her to put on her coat.) That second phone call separates the men husbands from the boy husbands. Nine out of ten wives think of one more item to buy as they hear you pulling out of the driveway, but by then it's too late to flag you down. In all likelihood she'll respond to this second phone call with relief. "My dearest husband, once again you have saved my life. A thousand thanks for calling. I forgot that I need a red cabbage and a jar of capers. You are a dream." Now wasn't her response well worth the call, especially if she's been annoyed at you lately for just cause?

This last call also allows you to double-check on any items on her list that the store might be out of, or to clarify exactly what she wants when it is unclear. Was it baking soda or baking powder? Does she want canned jellied cranberries or whole berries? They have no "new" potatoes. What alternative does she want?

A husband who arrives home after calling has taken that little extra step to make their union tighter. He has shown his wife that it is very important to him that she is pleased. And, he has conserved her strength, just a little bit, once again.

The Forbidden Food

One of the most important ways you can express your love for your wife is by kissing her. A kiss can communicate many different things to your mate—passion, affection, apology, forgiveness. In fact, kissing is perhaps the most important daily ingredient for nurturing warmth between a husband and a wife. Unfortunately, this effect is circumvented if care is not paid to whether or not your breath is fresh.

Even regular brushing and the use of a mouthwash can't neutralize the bad breath caused by eating certain foods, however—most notably, garlic. They say garlic is wonderful for your health, a miracle food. It enhances metabolism. It increases the absorption of vitamins. Garlic prevents parasites and slows the process of ageing. Garlic adds incredible flavor to virtually all foods. Garlic is natural.

My apologies to all the garlic growers, but eating garlic, in most cases, causes an awful mouth odor. Clients come into my office at eight o'clock in the morning reeking with foul breath. What have they possibly eaten so early in the day? Whatever happened to Corn Flakes? I've observed lovely women, magnificently coifed and impeccably dressed from head to toe, with a mouth odor so strong it completely overrides their elegant appearance. How can they be so unaware?

Garlic is horrible for your romantic health. How can you kiss someone who smells so bad? "But," protest the garlic fans, "if we both have garlic breath, then everything is okay." That's got to be one of the oddest observations ever. That's like saying, "She's repulsive. So, if I am repulsive too, then we can enjoy mutual repulsiveness." If you have no consideration for the human population which cohabit the earth with you, at least be merciful with the woman you love. Keep your kissing breath sweet.

Sharing Financial Decisions

What is this jazz about separate checking accounts, about allowances doled out from husband to wife, about his money and her money? The relationship between husband and wife is so close, so intense, so trusting, so united, that the separation of monetary assets should be absolutely unheard of (except perhaps when the assets of a family business or other special situations are involved). Marriage is not a business partnership or an everything-accounted-for public corporation. It is a loving, trusting union in which assets, rights, chattel, seat of power, and "I know best" attitudes don't belong.

Do you, the husband, know more than she does about checkbooks, arithmetic, interest rates, and monthly statements? Then teach her. Share it. She has taught you how to be a better father to your children. She has made your folks very comfortable in your home. She has helped deal with your social arrangements. Don't lock her out of the money area. You think you need two checking accounts because you both make out checks separately and there's only one checkbook? Then the one who makes out the most checks holds onto the checkbook and the other one records the checks he or she writes on a small card and transfers the information periodically—but the account stays joint!

There is also a mistaken notion that if he earns the money of the family with great effort and diligence, then he has earned the right to spend this money or invest it as he decides. There is something wrong with this reasoning. The responsibilities of the husband and wife—earning the money, bringing up the children, the laundry, the shopping, buying gifts, cleaning the house, etc.—are divided up, by mutual consent. Traditionally, though not necessarily, he will have the primary job and she will take care of the kids and the household needs. But, this arrangement is certainly not fixed in stone. When the wife has an outside job that is less flexible than her husband's, it is the husband who will be going to the parent-teacher conferences and the supermarket. The point is, earned money is their money, not his money. When it comes to investing, the decisions and choices must be theirs, not his. Many a man has made unwise choices in attempting to squeeze out that extra half point of interest and has squandered precious funds, subsequently altering the whole family's lifestyle. A wife (who cuts newspaper coupons and is forever looking for sales and specials) should discuss with her mate in detail the family money management issues, even if she doesn't know the commonly used terms on the financial pages. Her common sense will serve her just fine. Many wives would be shocked at what motivates their mates to make critical investment decisions—a tip from a co-worker, a convincing chance mailing, a *hunch!* These are the same mates who compare the price of diapers endlessly and complain about the spoiled leftovers neglected in the refrigerator (worth about thirty-two cents).

In marriages in which men give their wives a weekly allowance, this allowance should never be used as a power tool. The amount and the frequency are arrived at by discussion, on the basis of available funds and expected payment obligations. It should be totally flexible as new needs turn up. It is not his money versus her money, or "I paid for this, so you have to pay for that," or we'll "split the cost" of an upcoming vacation or a gift to a child. Holding the purse strings for power is a holdover from the Middle Ages. It is certainly not conducive to the ideal situation in which all major decisions affecting the family are shared.

Surprise Her

Without realizing it, men sometimes give more thought to what will please customers and family members—and even themselves—than they do to what will please their wives. Think about it. If we men have a waiting room at our place of business or profession, we think of details that will enhance it, such as a striking painting or free coffee or a bowl of hard candy for our visiting customers (details that hopefully will lead to added income). If we have a newborn child or grandchild, we impulsively purchase toys, mobiles, clothes, or books. If we love to garden, we find it hard to pass a store that sells things even vaguely connected to gardening without entering it to see what's new.

Well, if you think of treats for your customers, a new baby, or your precious garden, you should certainly be giving some thought to what might please the girl that you married. If something special catches your eye in a store, at a flea market, or any place where you spend your day, ask yourself, Would this please her? It need not be anything costly or dramatic like a Lexus or a mink coat. With big items, you're apt, justifiably, to take the time to compare prices or go to the library and research the item in *Consumer Reports*. However, it doesn't take a major purchase to bring a smile to your wife's face. Small items purchased spontaneously will brighten her day. It could be a little jar of rose hand cream found in a divinely scented sachet and perfume shop or a bouquet of bought wildflowers from a street vendor.

You might come across an antique eyeglass holder of handmolded brass to sit on her night table or a fragile crystal ring holder for the shelf above the sink where she can deposit her rings when she does laundry or the dishes. It could be one of these aluminum canes that opens, incredibly, into a portable seat that she can sit on when you go to a parade together. Maybe she'd be thrilled by some personalized stationery that you notice in a catalog while you're waiting at the printer to pick up your business cards.

Your wife will help you out by giving you clues as to what items she admires or would love to own. When she says, "Isn't that precious?" or "I just love that," your mental computer should pounce on whatever it is that she is referring to. That way, you have a running inventory to work from, which pretty well insures a pleased response to your gifts. Be selective about these surprise purchases, however. If you reach the point where every time your lady expresses her fondness for something, you get it for her, she might begin to feel uncomfortable. She might become afraid to say, "Oh, that's great!" about something she sees because, while it does please her, she doesn't actually want it for herself.

My wife was once so mesmerized by a fish tank set in a wall at the entrance of a restaurant that I literally had to pull her away from the tank when the busy hostess was ready to seat us. Needless to say, a couple of months later I surprised her with the largest fish tank a pet shop carried, together with filter, motor, fish, pebbles, and accessories. This surprise proved to be a disaster, on many counts. First, she had the job of maintaining the gift, which was really a handful for a mother with young children. Secondly, some of the aggressive fish started chasing and chomping on their more peaceful tankmates, which scared the wits out of the kids. The last straw came when two of the fish were found on the carpet dead one morning beneath the tank, having committed mutual hara-kiri by flipping themselves out of the water and over the side of the tank. Unfortunately, my gift to my lady did not include the weekly maintenance man the restaurant hired to service the tank, and the whole setup was sold a short time later.

Some treats will never fail to please her, and eventually you will learn the "instant winners." Who would have thought that a mere jelly donut, which you stopped to buy while dashing down the street for something else, would make her think that she has the most thoughtful husband in the whole world?

Have you read an interesting article recently? Cut it out and save it for her to enjoy. Crossing a bridge or tunnel? When you stop at the toll booth, pick up a roll of tokens for her car. When you're at the post office, buy a small book of stamps for her to slip into her wallet for home use. Do you regularly pass a library near your office? Pop in and pick up the book she wanted but never seemed to have the time to get for herself. Does she love caraway flavored rye bread or bagels but the stores are frequently out of them? Special order them from a bakery and surprise her with them when she's had a bad day.

Small surprises are an easy way to confirm your love for your wife. As noted before, all you have to do is listen very carefully. Over time, she will give you plenty of ideas as to how you can "surprise" her.

A Thoughtfully Chosen Card

There are at least two times a year, and often more, when you can bedazzle your beloved and make her heart soar by giving her a unique greeting card. These opportunities are on her birthday, your wedding anniversary, on Mother's Day if you are blessed with children, and really any other time that you want to transmit a message from your soul that will stir hers.

Here are a couple of suggestions if you want the reward of a delighted, appreciative smile on her face. First, do not give her a sarcastic card, such as one that reads, "Roses are blue, violets are red. This rhyme is twisted and so is your head."

Just as bad is one that states on the out-side, "Not everyone can be a mother like you!" and on the inside says, "You have to be female and at least 12 years old!" Save cards filled with wisecracks for the smart alecks in your office.

Secondly, do not give her a card that apologizes or even hints that there is even a question that your relationship is any-thing but the best one on earth and get-ting stronger every day. Too many cards imply gloom and doom between the lines and instill fear and pessimism about the future. They say, "Even in difficult times like this, I'm sure we can make it if we hang in strong together" or "Although we see around us couples splitting up, I know that if we respect our differences and give each other the space we each need, we have the potential of seeing this through."

Come on! These last two cards sound like messages between two total strangers. You and your wife are committed for life— unquestionably. Marriage is not a trial arrangement. It is a contract fixed in stone, and once it is accepted in this light, your messages and communications will reflect the work you put in to make this contract so sanctified and splendid that to be part of it is an absolute privilege.

So, what kind of card should you get? Well, pass up all the guffaw cards and cartoon cards and seasonal cards and Snoopy cards, and you'll find the area you're looking for in the back of the store, probably in a poorly lit area. It is a rack of greeting cards that all have sincere, sensitive messages, written in script, which gives the feeling of a personal, handwritten note. The headings of the messages are itemized by the subject and theme of the card, such as "Why I love you, Dearest" or "My Life Changed the Day I Met You" or "I Always Dreamt of Meeting Someone Like You" or "I'm Sorry" or "I Miss Our Closeness" or "How Can I Thank You?" Are these a joke or too corny to consider? No! Read them. You'll find many of them very well composed, with the knack of conveying the precise words that you would have written yourself if someone hadn't invented these cards.

Thumb through a bunch of them. The different nuances in the warm words give you a choice of messages, and very quickly you'll find one that is right on target. Grab it. You have something valuable in your hand. Your lady will be totally thrilled to receive it. You have my money-back guarantee.

Oh, by the way, you'll soon notice how lucky you are. The area of the store that houses this rack of cards is almost always empty. No one will bump into you. You will have all the time and privacy you need to choose the card that best expresses what it is that you want to say.

Two more pieces of advice. First, buy the cards a month (yes, a month) before the special day in question. It is a terrific feeling to have a great greeting card in your briefcase and be anxiously awaiting the day of delivery and the warm reception that your carefully chosen card will receive. In addition, you will never violate the cardinal rule of forgetting an important occasion if you are well prepared in advance. (The assumption here is that you are well organized with a daily diary that you lean on like a private secretary. At the beginning of the year, all critical dates should be recorded in it. The notation to purchase a card should be entered approximately a month in advance on the appropriate daily page.) There is nothing sadder than overhearing a woman say, "Oh, I got lovely cards from the family. My husband? He never remembers our anniversary."

Last, write a short personal note or comment at the bottom of the card before you sign it. Although the printed message already says it so well, adding a few words of your own will make the card even more meaningful.

It doesn't take a lot of money to show your wife how much you care about her. A thoughtfully chosen card for no particular occasion will make her feel enormously loved and appreciated. It's a simple act, but it's one that will mean a lot to her.

Chapter Eight

Spending Time Alone

In our busy lives, the opportunities for a man and woman to talk seriously and without interruption for a decent length of time are very few and precious. Every couple needs time, however, for the kind of deep, intimate conversations that foster a close relationship.

When going to a restaurant with your wife, alone, pick a restaurant that has the optimum atmosphere for focused communication. This focused communication should be your highest priority on this excursion, not the food. The meal should be something you both will enjoy, but it is secondary when selecting a restaurant for just you and your wife. You want to whisper and giggle with your romantic partner, and you need a special setting.

Do not select a restaurant with loud music. (Any time you see people around very loud music and apparently happy, you know that they have selected not to communicate with whomever they are with.) Ideally, the tables should not be too close together either. Loud and agitated conversation, while perfectly normal, can be very distracting when it's too close. And, after all, if you want to sneak in a quick kiss or lean over and rub noses, you'll feel less inhibited without an audience. (Booths are great. You are locked into your own private cable car!)

Do not go to an eatery where you're apt to know people. Eating out with someone ought to be a private session. Unfortunately, this seems to be a minority opinion. The sweetest people will come over to you in a restaurant—just when you're at the point of resolving a difficult impasse with your wife or just when you're relating the climax of an amazing adventure you've just experienced—and they will stand over you, surprisingly ready for a long chat. Invariably, instead of a quick hello and good-bye, their opening greeting will be "So, what good movies have you seen lately?" or "What are your children doing this summer?" Now, don't get me wrong. There is plenty of room in life for going out to eat with friends and blabbing away for hours. What we are discussing here is different. The two of you have elected to be alone in order to spend quality time together. It must not be diluted.

The Final Detail

So, you've picked the right place. It's off the beaten track, so you probably won't bump into anyone you know. If you've selected well, the lighting will be dim; candlelight is the greatest. (It is amazing how many establishments still persist in having fluorescent lighting. I guess the insurance is less expensive if there are no lit candles anywhere.) There is soft, gentle, pleasing music. The seating is spread out, and there are a few isolated groups or couples sprinkled around the large room, giving a feeling of peace.

Pick the last table in the farthest corner. Have your wife sit with her back to the wall, while you sit across from her with your back to the rest of the restaurant. As my mother used to say, "If you have a diamond, put it in the best setting." If her back is to the wall, there is no movement going on behind her to distract you so you can give your full attention to what she is saying. By sitting across from one another, you are looking into each other's eyes and concentrating on your communication. It is here that solving problems, planning events, discussing the children, dreaming, and just plain cooing, are best accomplished. (Oddly enough, many people select a strange seating arrangement in certain food establishments, a kind of scalloped curved seating along the walls facing the center of the room, where it's virtually impossible to face your partner. The couple ends up almost side-by-side facing the entire room—the moving waiters, the entering customers, the dessert cart, and the cashier. They face everyone and everything except themselves. How in the world are they going to conduct business and whisper romantic messages when there is no eye-to-eye contact?)

Occasionally, you will run into someone else as intent on landing the perfect table as you are. He discovers the same seats you want and ends up competing with you for them! This can be very inconvenient, but it really gives me a chuckle to find that there is someone else out there who is just as dogged in his thinking and planning as I am. The best defense against this is to get the number of the table you want from the waiter so you can call in beforehand and reserve the table by its number for a certain time.

This system can also fail on occasion, however, when two other people are seated there earlier in the evening, an apparently "safe" two and a half hours before your scheduled reservation. When you arrive at 8:30, they're still there and are still going strong! They have lost all track of time. Well . . . if you're a regular customer, and if the hostess is fairly astute, and if you look helpless enough, and if it looks like they won't get up until the house lights go out, and if you mentally will it hard enough, the two squatters on your site might be gently and diplomatically coaxed into leaving by the restaurant personnel. If not, a sense of humor and the next best table in the house are in order. After all, you still have the soft music and the candlelight. Make the most of the opportunity you've created to spend some quality time alone with your wife.

The Weekly Envelope

With the premise that your wife is your best friend, your soul mate, and your partner in everything on this earth, you must know everything about her life and she about yours. Your individual thoughts, plans, disappointments, projects, victories, dreams, and worries have to be exchanged at regularly scheduled, quality time sessions. This is the only way to accomplish the extreme closeness that you both desire. If both of you are leading busy, active, productive lives, however, these communication sessions are at a premium. For couples who can't manage the Tuesday-Wednesday getaway suggested later, the next best thing is to set aside time each week to spend exclusively with one another.

The question is, How do you remember all the thoughts and feelings of the whole week, plus all the minutiae on your agenda, without forgetting most of it by the time your designated day comes rolling along? How can you realistically recall each item from the previous week that you wanted to ask your wife about?

It is true that on a given evening, after a pressure-filled workday, after eating, after hugging the kids and catching up on the highlights of their day, after phone calls, after errands, after bathing, and before conking out for the night, there are moments available for a husband and wife to converse. But, these moments are so few and so brief, that the communication can only cover the most critical subjects that have to be dealt with immediately, without the detail, the background, the implications, and the feelings behind these subjects. The car developed a terrible noise today every time the brakes were used. A relative is in the hospital and must be visited within the next day and a half. Your wife had a horrible argument with someone in her office. One of your kids lost the loose-leaf book containing her term project. Are we interested in buying the last two tickets for an upcoming theater party? Do we have some room in our car to take two more people to Sunday's wedding?

These items, and many others, are quickly administered to and dealt with. They are a part of life. Delving into the details and the feelings they elicit will have to wait until your designated catch-up day.

A suggestion is presented here on how not to lose even one detail of what went on during the previous week in either of your lives. Write them all down on your desk calendar or daily work diary. If Tuesday is your designated day, put down everything on the page for that day. How was your wife's conversation with her cousin? Jot down a reminder to sign up for an adult education course. Which is the best week this spring to visit Amsterdam? Tell me about your bad dream the other night. When is the tile man coming back to finish up the floor? We need baby gifts for three babies born this week. When are you going for your annual checkup? Remember that we have parent-teacher conferences next week. You need some new ties. You embarrassed me the other day at the party and you weren't even aware. I love your haircut. Did you hear the latest joke?

There is so much to share and think about for a working team, and this full page in your diary is only for one week! It takes just a second to record a feeling or idea because you can quickly flip to the diary page and write it down. The items that have to be reviewed two weeks or two months in the future are simply put down on the designated page for that particular week.

On the eve of your exclusive day together, transfer all the items on the diary page to the back of a long envelope. This alleviates the need to carry your work briefcase or daily diary with you. It also gives you a chance to review your agenda before you get together with your wife. After all, many of the items on the page will have been transferred from weeks or even months ago and have been almost forgotten. The envelope should also have an area for excursions or errands if you are able to arrange an afternoon or a whole day together, whether it be looking at a new kitchen table or stopping at the photographer or dropping off a gift for your granddaughter.

Remember the line in the movie *Jaws*, "We need a bigger boat"? Well, if your long envelope is not full, you are not sharing enough with your wife. Have you covered all her hobbies and stories about the children and her problematic relationships? The ideal is for you to use the entire envelope and wish you had a bigger one. (And, you'll be surprised how much you'll have to share with your wife once you get into the habit of writing these things down.) At the end of your day together the entries that were dealt with are crossed off, and the ongoing ones are transferred to a future page in your diary.

I'm always saddened when I hear about a married couple who drive together for hours in complete silence. It means that they are living separate lives or that they are sharing most of their intimate thoughts and experiences with someone else. Just as disheartening to me are couples who always invite company on their drives so that they won't have to be alone together, or couples who listen to long cassette tapes on the trip, or couples in which the nondriving mate sleeps for most of the trip. All of these are okay, if the communication that ought to be forthcoming has already been mutually shared, and they are all "talked out" and content. But, when these "silent partners" can't or won't share with each other, they need guidance (professional or otherwise), for they might be living together but missing out on the potential for a close, warm, connected relationship.

Chapter Nine

The Tuesday-Wednesday Getaway

If at all possible, a husband and wife should spend a weekday or at least half a day together each week, alone and away-y-y-y. (A weekend day doesn't count because the kids are off from school. There are also social obligations, religious requirements, relatives to see, and shopping to do. Saturdays and Sundays are indeed "family" days.) Admittedly, job obligations, cost considerations, and the needs of your children often make this an unrealistic wish. But, don't give up. If a couple wants this day for themselves badly enough, and they are persistent and imaginative and even willing to forego precious income, they might be able to find a way to attain it.

Sometimes, instead of working the usual eight hours a day, five days a week, you can arrange to work ten hours a day, four days a week, and thus free up a day. Sometimes, if you look hard enough, you can find a relative, trustworthy friend, or neighbor whom your kids love that you can pay to watch your children while you're away. Sometimes, the idea that there are certain imperative matters that only you personally can take care of is just a fixed idea in your head.

No one is indispensable. Even a farmer who milks his cows twice a day has to get someone to fill in for him on the day that he has to go into town to get a haircut, or vote, or do whatever farmers do in town. Anyway, getting away during the week is such a monumental prize that it is worth turning the world upside down, losing money, and being liked by a few less people, to achieve.

And (are you ready for this?), when finances, work, children, hobbies, and community allow it, make it an overnight getaway. The best combination is probably from Tuesday after work until Wednesday around supper time. It breaks up the week. (If you find it absolutely impossible to arrange a regular overnight getaway, strive for at least two full weekend getaways a year, and schedule one of these on your wedding anniversary.)

First and foremost, what about the kids? Well, you have already racked your brains and have come up with a suitable sitter, so adding a night just means more clever thinking and arranging. Although the kids may complain at first, in time they will get used to the idea and eventually even look forward to an evening without parental pressures, especially if it is accompanied by some well-chosen special privileges and treats. What often works well is to take the kids out to dinner every Wednesday night after you return, a "mini-party" for just the two of you and your kids. Over this meal in a restaurant, your children will have a chance to show you their school projects, their graded tests, their scraped knees, the rips in their best jackets, and how tall they got since you left yesterday afternoon. They can complain about who hit them in school, how much homework they had to do without you, and how mean the baby sitter was. They can confess that your favorite frame was broken while you were away because it was, after all, too close to the edge of the coffee table, and they're sure that missing the school bus that morning was not their fault—probably the bus came too early. You will have a chance to give them your undivided attention. After hearing them out thoroughly, you will wisely give them each some delectable souvenir you picked up while you were away.

At home later that evening, you will hug them thoroughly, give them quantity and quality time, and patiently put them to bed with a great story. Thus, you've made Wednesday night, the night after your Tuesday night, a weekly celebration with the kids that they, and you, can joyously look forward to. You've turned a negative (your absence) into a positive (a party night). If possible, this Wednesday night routine with your children should be as untouchable and predictable as your Tuesday night with your wife is.

Of course, despite the best laid plans, things do happen. (Why do they always seem to fall on a Tuesday-Wednesday?) As an example, my daughter received a graded test back on a Tuesday afternoon with instructions from the teacher that it be signed by her parents that night and returned to school the next day. My daughter returned the unsigned test back to the teacher, explaining that, regretfully, her parents were away and thus could not sign it. No problem. The very next Tuesday afternoon my daughter received another graded test from the same teacher, again to be signed that night by a parent. My daughter, sensing disaster, immediately declared that it would be impossible to get the test signed because her parents would be away again that night. The teacher (who obviously couldn't conceive of the idea of regular romantic interludes) exploded at my daughter, called her a liar, accused her of hiding things from her parents, and warned her that she could not come back to class the next day unless she had a signed test with her or the teacher heard from one of her parents.

Well, as usual, we called home that night (a safety measure we always practiced), and listened to the tearful recounting of the story. Fortunately, we were able to save the day with a minimum of time and effort. Living two houses from our home was a friend who was a teacher in the same school. We phoned her. She thought the whole thing was adorable. She took my daughter with her when she went to work at school the next morning, explained everything to the teacher involved, and everyone lived happily ever after.

I used to humor my children by telling them that I would give them a signed "blanket" note before I went away, which would say something like this: "I am writing this note to say that what my child did today was absolutely awful, and I give you my word that I thoroughly reprimanded her, and this regrettable behavior will never be repeated." I never actually gave my kids such a letter, but they enjoyed the idea immensely, and it gave them greater confidence during our absence.

Setting Out

Your wife has left a long list of instructions for the baby sitter, prepared the children's clothes for the next day, called close relatives to be on alert in case of emergency, swallowed hard at the prospect of deserting job, house, and children, and is now ready to switch identities from mother to romantic lover. (Leaving overnight is usually more difficult for a mother than for a father, but once the kids get older and the kinks in the preparation are ironed out, the separation process gradually becomes much easier.)

You have, likewise, rearranged your routine aggressively and relentlessly. You have worked a very long Monday and an average Tuesday; you are scheduled to work a very long Thursday. You've promised the kids all sorts of goodies that they can expect when you return, in addition to the Wednesday restaurant supper party. You've packed your suitcase. You are now ready for your rendezvous. Where should you go?

It is recommended that you travel to a destination thirty to sixty minutes away, for a few reasons. First of all, it's far enough from home and/or work to let you forget about your routine and feel like you're in a deliciously new, refreshing area. It should not be more than an hour because, after all, you are returning late the next afternoon, so the driving shouldn't be a burden. Also, since the trip might be repeated fifty times a year, rain or snow or ice will not put a damper on your getaway if you don't travel too far. Depending on the season, how you expect to spend Wednesday often determines your destination. A small town in the "country" near a metropolitan area is ideal for most Wednesday options (for instance, a small New England village in Connecticut located a short distance from the New York City area).

Pick a romantic inn, one with landscaped grounds and a special quaint atmosphere. The inn shouldn't be expensive—just clean, charming, and conducive to cuddling. Look for a room with flowered wallpaper, frilly upholstery, a working fireplace, and a four-poster bed draped with lace all around.

The room should have nothing modern, with the possible exception of a phone and maybe a TV. The sink should be small, with antique knobs and faucets. The bathroom might even be "on the floor" down the hall, a reminder of camp, college, and your single days.

After your arrival, set aside some time to unwind before you do anything else. Instead of turning on the TV, try relaxing with a hot bath and an hour or two of reading or napping. This can be followed by a leisurely dinner in a setting where the two of you can sit across from one another without any strong distractions. Avoid people seated too close to your table, smoke, loud music, and being rushed. This is your time together with the outside world shut out, sharing dreams and thoughts, working on problems— working on your relationship.

Sleep late on Wednesday morning (if you are fortunate enough not to have an automatic inner alarm clock). Look out the windows. Open them and enjoy the trees, the birds, the flowers, the sky, and the fresh country air. Amble downstairs in your slippers and robe or something else comfortable to the breakfast nook. If you're lucky, there will be a continental breakfast included. (What a wonderful term *continental breakfast* is. Although it is usually modest, it always seems to have the promise of style and grace and fine serving pieces; of gentle background music and other thoughtful touches that make you feel like a pampered guest. Even the words they use on the little signs around the serving table at many inns seem more appealing than those found in your neighborhood diner: *scones, currants, preserves, croissants, pop-overs, tarts, almonds* [never "nuts"], *fresh boysenberries.*)

Your taste buds are alive again. Look around. Listen to the soft, classical music. Savor the peacefulness of your surroundings. Enjoy this time alone with the woman who works as hard as you do during the rest of the week (and she does, whether she's a full-time homemaker or has a job of her own outside the home).

After breakfast, you have more hours to read, enjoy the fireplace, relax, nap, walk, and talk until midday when you check out.

An inn like this, whether it is always the same one or a rotation of a few favorites, can be perfect during the months of October through April. Warmer weather provides even more options, like camping in a tent or little villas with sprawling gardens to explore. Rent a cottage by a lake and go canoeing, or just sit on the porch side-by-side and enjoy the view.

Wednesday Afternoons

Ask your wife what she would like to do—it's her day. Men usually have more freedom and options during the rest of the week than women do, so spend Wednesday doing something she enjoys. Do not go off golfing or fishing someplace alone, even if your wife encourages you to. She wants to please you, but remember, this is a mini-honeymoon, not your personal day off.

If the weather is nice, see if she'd like to spend the day outdoors. Teach her how to put a worm on a hook. Cross a rushing stream, stepping carefully on those slippery wet rocks—but do it holding hands. Ask her which flowers or birds are her favorites and then look for them together. Ride bikes with her on those wondrous, narrow, curving country roads. Stop and ponder over an unusual tree, a grazing horse, or somebody's nearby dream house. Visit a local museum or a historic house. Suggest a matinee if the feature is one you know she'll enjoy.

Chilly Wednesday afternoons? These are great for doing something athletic, like ice skating or skiing. There are usually small neighborhood skiing areas around the suburbs that only the locals know about. These are never advertised or crowded and are often a relatively short drive from your overnight location. It might be pointed out that when you are having "leaf fights" with your wife on a crisp Wednesday afternoon in late October, or watching the college crew teams sculling across a lake, most of the rest of the world is working. Traffic is usually light, the stores are nearly empty, the usual long lines for amusements that are packed on weekends and holidays aren't there at all. Everything seems casual. You can enjoy the recreation areas almost privately, and play with a casual, relaxed abandon. The world for you two is your own exclusive playground.

In the winter, don't overlook sledding as a great, free, widely available activity that brings romantic couples closer and makes them feel refreshingly young and vibrant. A prepared husband will have the following items in his car trunk throughout the whole winter: Ski-type jackets with hoods or a warm hat, gloves, waterproof overshoes, boots, his pair of ice skates and hers, and two sleds. Don't remove these items from the trunk until the crocuses finish blooming!

Sleds are inexpensive and virtually indestructible. For the very thrifty, used sleds can be found at most flea markets for under five dollars each. Choose sledding hills with increasing levels of fright and length if you are daring. Go down together on one sled, either sitting one in front of the other, or one lying on top of the other, head first. Or, use two sleds and make up some mildly competitive games, like seeing who can keep the sled moving the longest. Sled until you're exhausted and your cheeks are rosy—or you're tired out from just giggling. It's a good way to end the day, and after a cup of hot chocolate or an indoor swim, you're invigorated and thawed out and ready for the drive home.

Don't forget to make lunch on Wednesday a special, shared treat. Instead of going to a diner, do something unusual. Order room service and eat on the balcony outdoors at the inn if it's warm enough. Have a picnic at the edge of a sparkling brook. (Of course, don't buy the food at a supermarket. Go together to the general store of a little town. These places sell virtually everything, and they have the unique flavor of an era long gone by.)

Eat in the car beside a lake filled with geese and experience the fun (or annoyance) of their strutting up to your car and even banging on the car door with their beaks, looking for a handout. Eat in a crowded ski lodge, even if you didn't ski there. The food is usually inexpensive, the views are great, and you won't have to stuff your feet into those blasted ski boots. The important thing is that you and your wife spend a relaxing, carefree day together, the way you did when the two of you were dating.

When it's over, you'll feel rejuvenated, as if you were away for five full days instead of twenty-four hours—and next Tuesday is only six days away.

This overnight getaway, if experienced regularly, is guaranteed to establish a tight, cohesive marital relationship. It's not merely a vacation. It is an opportunity for a man to get to know every detail of his woman's existence. How did she spend her days this week? To whom did she speak? What worries her? health? children? relationships? You have the quantity time, as well as the quality time you need. You can say, "Tell me about your day" or "Tell me what you think about." You can review upcoming social engagements and household items that have to be repaired, as well as some of the issues between you and your wife that could stand repairing, too.

You can giggle together, play games, explore, plan, rehash, and recall nice memories. You have a relaxed setting in which to review changes you'd like to see in your relationship, or in your partner and vice versa, without worrying about time, pressure, or privacy. By taking this time out from the daily routine every week, you're not just giving lip service to working on your friendship; you're actually doing the nitty-gritty groundwork. You are saying that your relationship with your wife is foremost in terms of your priorities.

When two individuals marry, they must learn to deal not only with the common differences between any two people, but also with the conflicts of their original families, each of which has differing customs, values, and outlooks. It is hard to smooth out all the rough edges that are inevitable when any two people are thrown so closely together. A regularly scheduled getaway, however, provides you with an opportunity to work on your marriage without it feeling like work.

You and your wife will become best friends, with a myriad of shared experiences that will bring you closer together. You will be soul mates, comfortable enough with each other to share your most intimate thoughts. You will laugh and cry together and arrive at the point where you'll think of the same thought separately and be amazed that even your thoughts are unified.

I am often surprised when I hear a husband ask his wife, "When do you get off from work on Thursdays, honey?" or "When does your holiday vacation start?" or "Where did you go to high school?" I wonder why he doesn't know the answers. Sometimes these people have been married for years, yet the questions sound like those asked between two strangers who barely know each other.

If you're going to be together with the same person from your twenties until at least your eighties or nineties, it might as well be with someone you understand and know all about, and who feels the same way about you. The togetherness you foster when you set aside regular time to spend with your wife makes this the most rewarding hobby you can have.

Occasional Glitches

Pitfalls await every couple who reserve Tuesday evening and Wednesday for each other—good pitfalls and unfortunate pitfalls. Important events in life sometimes happen on your scheduled twenty-four hour getaway. Family weddings, emergencies, deaths, and graduations will occur. The family dog might decide to get sick on a Tuesday night, or maybe one Wednesday, your son is being honored at an assembly and every single parent in the whole class will be there. What should you do? Well, for emergencies or sad occasions, of course you have to be there. For the other type of conflicts, however, everything is negotiable!

Barter and trade. Can the baby sitter take the dog to the vet? (You'll compensate her for her trouble and the kids will relish the extra excitement during your absence.) It's the fourth month in a row that your son has been recognized as one of the honor roll students in his class. Can you throw him a celebratory skating party on the weekend and get your parents or his favorite aunt to attend the assembly on your behalf?

Alas, when a close relative calls you at 5:00 P.M. on a Tuesday afternoon, ecstatically announcing that his long-awaited first child was just born; that mother and child thankfully are doing very well; and that you were the very first one he called, friend or relative, because he knew that you would be as absolutely thrilled with the wonderful news as the parents themselves and would want to see the baby immediately—get a grip on yourself. Summon up your warmest, most ecstatic tone and thank him, from the bottom of your heart, for even thinking of you at this historic moment, when he has so much on his mind and heart. After all, people you care about are not blessed with new babies every day of the week. Cancel your overnight reservations (but not the baby sitter!) and reserve a late-night table for you and your wife at your favorite restaurant. You still want to hear all about her week, and you still have an envelope filled with thoughts and ideas that you want to share with her.

Although you'll sometimes have to forfeit a planned overnight getaway, do your best to salvage every one that you can. Consider carefully if what you're cancelling your getaway for is more important than the time you've scheduled to spend with your wife (and no, free tickets to a playoff game—even a championship one—don't qualify as more important). Those regularly scheduled catch-up days are doing more to strengthen your marriage than you realize.

Chapter Ten

Treat Her with Great Respect

Picture the scenario. Your wife has cooked dinner for her family. This could be a special holiday meal or simply a supper during the week. Guests might be present or your family might be eating alone. She could be serving you right on the kitchen table or bringing the food from the kitchen into the dining room. The food—delicious, hot, and appetizing—is set down in front of you, and the incredible aroma makes your mouth water. In my opinion, it is an act of respect on the part of you, the husband, and any children whose behavior you oversee, not to pick up your fork or spoon to eat until your wife is seated at the table ready to eat with you.

In many families, you will observe that as soon as the wife serves her husband his bowl of soup, he will put his head down, gobble up the soup, and not come up for air until he has finished the last drop. In all likelihood, the same behavior is practiced by the children and any guests who are present. This pattern continues with each subsequent course of the meal. By the time the wife sits down to eat, her man has finished that particular course and is impatiently ready for the next course. Sometimes he will wolf down his main course as soon as she serves him then leave the room—gone by the time she gets to sit down and eat.

There are several different reasons why "servees" begin to eat before the server sits down herself. Often, that's the way it was done in the home where the husband grew up. No one waited for his mother, so it feels perfectly natural to him to act this way. For some, it's just an instinctive behavior to begin eating anything set down on the table in front of them if they're very hungry. Sometimes, the husband is in a rush to finish the meal so he can get to the next thing—work, play, or a TV program he's anxious to watch.

At times it is the wife herself who creates the situation. She'll announce that the food is hot and ready and the family shouldn't wait for her or the food will get cold. Or, perhaps she has lots of items to bring in from the serving area before she's ready to sit. If you're all waiting for her, she feels compelled to rush through the serving process instead of taking her time serving the food that she spent so much time preparing. To avoid that pressure, she urges everyone to start eating without her.

Forget it! Don't listen to her. A loving husband, together with the children and guests seated with him at the table, should wait until she is comfortably seated before they begin eating. If, indeed the food is hot and many people are being served, or there are many items to be brought to the table, a good husband and his children (some of whom are future husbands themselves) should be right in the kitchen giving her a hand with the work so that she can enjoy eating the meal with them.

It is up to you, the husband, to set a rule in your house that anyone eating at your table must wait for your wife to join you. Enforcing the rule is not always that simple, however, especially with guests. With your own children, the rule is understood, because, since the beginning of their existence, you have impressed upon them the respect with which their mother must be treated. They are used to your reminders that "this is not a cafeteria" or "Please go into the kitchen and ask your mother how you can assist her."

As far as the guests go, allowances sometimes have to be made. If they are first-time guests at your table, they might be caught by surprise with an embarrassing mouthful of food before they realize that you and your children are waiting for your wife. On the other hand, if the guests are frequent visitors or "new" relatives, like a new son- or daughter-in-law, then it's all right to make the house policy known. It often can be conveyed by indirect communication or a subtle gesture. An example of indirect communication would be the following scenario.

You are sitting with your familiar guests, and your wife brings in the entree on a platter, which she places near one of the guests. That guest immediately starts to pass the platter to you at the head of the table as a courtesy. This gives you the opportunity to say, "It's all right. I'll wait for my wife to come in before I start eating." If instead of offering you the platter, the guest simply begins loading up his or her plate, the inappropriateness of this action will usually register when the guest realizes that no one else at the table is doing the same. Sometimes a gesture by you toward the kitchen where your wife is still fussing with the final touches of the meal will subtly convey the message to your guest.

In any event, it is incumbent upon you, the husband, to set the example. Help her in the kitchen. Wait until she joins you at the table. She has made an effort to make the meal just so, but she is not a waitress or a cook. She is your partner in life. Treat her as such.

In Public, Only Praise

Your respect for your wife should be as evident in public as it is in your home. Unfortunately, it is commonplace in social situations for men to put down their wives in order to get a laugh. "Oh, to my wife, the financial page of the newspaper is written in Chinese." "My wife? She's always losing things." Some use slang terms for their wives to accentuate "jokes."

"My old lady? Nice house but nobody's home!" You hear this talk so frequently that it almost sounds normal. Most male stand-up comics feast upon the wives in their routines. "For a weekend vacation, I'll pack only two pairs of clean under-wear into my pockets and there she is with four big suitcases. She says that it may get cold. It may get very cold. It may get almost cold. It may be windy. It may be very windy. It may be medium windy..." Or, "My wife overdresses so much, the other day she tripped while walking on her spike heels, but her fall was broken when she landed on her false eyelashes."

Well, all this chitchat is good for co-medians who earn a living making fun of wives, celebrities, and presidents, but for a loving husband, it is a no-no. Remem-ber my mother's saying, "If you have a fine diamond, place it in the best setting"? Well, if you have a fine lady, you must always surround her with a setting of ad-miring words and feelings. It is not enough to be cuddly together when you're alone at home in front of a fireplace. The affec-tion you exhibit privately must be ex-tended to public situations. Compliment her publicly (although not in excess, to avoid making her or the listeners uneasy) and be positive when relating stories about her.

What if you are at odds with each other at home, or both upset about a problem you haven't had time to resolve before being thrust into the public eye? Don't reveal this private disagreement in front of others, either by your words or your actions. Be pleasant and diplomatic. It might take some effort, but you should always keep your displeasure with one another private. Whether you realize it or not, other married couples publicly hide their anger at one another all the time! In this area, husbands and wives are the world's best actors. If you and your wife can set aside your differences for the moment, it will prevent the tension between you from marring the social occasion. More important, it will give the two of you time to let your emotions subside a little before you discuss the matter again.

So, until the festering wound is healed, fake it in the presence of others. Treat your wife as your beloved, even if you're hurt inside. To the rest of the world, what you say about her must always be complimentary. Then, when alone, do your homework together and clean up the mess.

In public, be positive. Be gallant. Be proud of her.

Voice Your Appreciation

We all have egos, and our egos all
need stroking. We need words that make
us feel good and give us confidence and
validation. At times we depend on the
input of others to pump us up, to give us
security and a feeling of self-worth. A wife
is no different. She might breeze along,
day in and day out, caring for the kids,
maintaining her job, doing the laundry,
turning out the meals, and making it look
like these accomplishments are effortless
and second nature to her. They are, but
they're not.

She's doing them because she wants
you and the children to be happy and
high-functioning without having to be hin-
dered with most of the chores necessary
for running a household. Acknowledge her
good deeds. Be openly appreciative of all
she does for you and your family.

Make it your business to thank her
every day, at least a few times, for the
many things that she does which please
you or make your life easier. Make it your
business to know what she has accomplished every day. Your wife might have
spent an hour on your armoire, removing
all the sweaters (curled up and thrown
in), checking them, folding them neatly,

and returning them to their place. There's nothing earth-shattering in this, but it took time. Take the time to thank her for it. She might have spent another hour on your bookcase, lining up the books and cassettes and videos neatly, and discarding some duplicated items and unimportant junk mail. Tell her you noticed and that you appreciate what she did.

She might have called your relatives because you're always too busy. She might have sent out birthday cards to your two nieces whose birthdays are coming up this weekend. She might have spent a whole afternoon going through one of your children's closets and drawers, pulling out all the items that they have outgrown, which need to be given away. She might have spent valuable time fixing a fallen cuff on your pants or looking for a missing button or trying to reach your key that fell behind a heavy dresser and was virtually inaccessible. Thank her whenever you have the opportunity.

It is mind-boggling and indeed very sad that there are marriages in which appreciation is not regularly expressed. An unthanked mate becomes discouraged. In many of these cases, a husband simply doesn't realize that his wife needs some sign from him that he appreciates her. Sooner or later, the wife will become resentful, and it won't be long before her resentment surfaces. Hopefully, she will be wise enough and strong enough to teach her husband, early in the marriage what constitutes appropriate acknowledgment. A good wife fills in all the gaps and smoothes out all the rough edges in their daily life. This is one of the ways that "every wise woman buildeth her house" (Prov. 14:1). That's part of her job. "Thanks again, dear."

And, intermittently, give your wife a higher form of thanks. "Thank you for marrying me." "Thank you for being mine." "Thank you for being."

Encourage Closeness with Her Relatives

Much richness in life comes from our relationships with our relatives—grandparents, parents, siblings, aunts and uncles, nieces and nephews, children and grandchildren. We share joyous and sad occasions with them. We have a lifetime connection to them, for better or worse, and they, plus the friends and acquaintances whom we select, combine to make up the minisociety in which we travel through life.

The relationship with these individual relatives is often very complicated, fraught with difficult histories, rivalries, jealousies, secrets, resentments, disappointments, and anxieties. Unraveling these complicated and negative feelings often takes years to accomplish.

Your partner in life brings into your union her family members and where she stands with each of them, the good stuff and the bad stuff. She has her agenda with each of them, those that bring positive feelings and those that bring out the negative. Some of her relatives might be good buddies while some might have been written off by her. She might long to be close to some. She might be going through great suffering with others.

As a caring husband, you should give your woman unconditional support as she works out these relationships. Your own biases should be subjugated if they interfere with what she is trying to accomplish. Always, always, encourage closeness with her family members. Dealing with related individuals can be extremely difficult, so give her all the upbeat assistance you can. Don't make her fight you in addition to fighting them. Often you cannot comprehend her deep-seated feelings.

The rewards gained from family successes, large and small, are potentially enormous. These are the people who represent where you and your wife each came from, why you are as you are, where you are going, and the legacy you're both going to leave on this earth.

Encourage difficult phone calls. Encourage the uncomfortable conversations that often are necessary to clear the air. Be eager to visit her relatives and open your house to them, even the "impossible" ones. Especially when it comes to her siblings and parents, be supportive of the work needed to effectuate closeness.

Be there for her.

Always Part with Affection

We're all familiar with the admonition that a husband and wife should never end a day in anger. The manner in which they begin their day is equally important, however. When you separate in the morning to spend the balance of the day apart, your good-bye to your wife should be a warm kiss. Sometimes you're still asleep, and she's off and running. At other times she's asleep and you're flying out to make the 6:45 train. Sometimes she's helping the kids get ready for school, and you're about to be picked up by your car pool.

You should give her, not only a kiss, but a slow cheek-to-cheek nuzzle. This little gesture is like a reaffirmation of your closeness and your marriage bond before you separate for a whole day to deal with the world individually. It is a reminder that you are loyally bound to each other, even when you're on your own, and that your pact is more important than that which you hope to accomplish during the day. It is a tiny act of warmth to sustain you until you're rejoined in the evening.

The good-bye kiss also is a statement of closeness to each other if you went to bed separately the night before for one reason or another, or if you ended the previous day with some irritation between you that was not completely resolved. It says that even though you need to catch up on your communication, you are still very, very connected.

In a subtle way, your good-bye kiss also teaches your kids the importance of a close relationship between man and wife. For years, whenever our kids kissed their mother good-bye before getting on the school bus in the mornings, they smelled my after-shave fragrance on her, and they told us so. (The moral of the story is that you'd better keep kissing, because when-

ever you stop, the children will be the
first to know!)

Your Marriage Is a Legacy

Fair warning: How you treat your wife
and how the two of you get along together as a couple will have a strong impact on at least the next two generations
(just as how you act today is very much
influenced by and determined by the past
behavior of your parents and grandparents). What your son sees in your house
will be the basis of what he perceives as
normal. He will perpetuate this image
when he, in turn, finds a wife and sets up
his home. In your son's home, his son—
your grandson—will be learning from his
father what is deemed to be normal and
acceptable.

Likewise, your daughters will absorb
how your wife is treated by you. When
they date, they will have as their frame of
reference their mother and her marriage.
So, when it comes to selecting mates of
their own, your children will (consciously
or unconsciously) picture the relationship
between their father and mother.

The enormous responsibility of being
a great husband does not end with the
impact it has on your wife. It is known

that a happy marriage is more apt to produce happy and well-adjusted children, children who will do well with friendships and schooling and values. In addition, your son will seek to marry a girl whom he can take care of, one who will love him intensely and who will be equally insistent on a tight marital relationship.

Your daughter will not just settle for someone who only supports her financially and is "good" to her. She is going to demand the best. She's going to expect her husband to regularly set aside time to spend alone with her. She's going to insist on marrying a guy who appreciates the value of romance in his marriage.

Your children will learn that regular hard work is necessary for a marriage to thrive. They will learn that money cannot buy love. They will learn that quantity time, as well as quality time, is essential for closeness. They will have instilled in them the importance of respect, caring, humor, and romance. Hopefully, you and your wife will be exceptional role models for the next (and the next) generation.

Chapter Eleven

Have Fun Together

Since your wife is your best friend and you are destined to spend much time with her alone, the times you spend together should be fun. There should be heavy doses of humor and silliness, and not just during the early years of marriage. A couple can giggle together into their nineties. They not only love each other, but they like each other. They have found ways to keep their marriage fun. Look for pastimes you and your wife can enjoy together. There are board games, like Scrabble, and athletic games like tennis. Some couples are just competitive enough to keep the contest interesting, while some mates take winning or losing far more seriously.

Extreme competitiveness between marital partners is counterproductive, however. It brings out certain combative strategies, such as taking advantage of the other's weakness, devising ways to outsmart or deceive or simply thinking of your opponent as the enemy. These feelings, to me, are not consistent with loving kindness, gentle support, and just rooting for each other—feelings that your relationship tries to maximize.

The games best suited to lovers are focused less on winning and score keeping than on making us think or laugh. They're often mental gymnastics, suitable for time spent sitting on a beach together, or word games that make the time pass pleasantly on a long car trip or while standing in line. Think up trivia questions to ask one another. These can pertain to topics of general interest or be more personal in nature. See which one of you can remember the names of all of your elementary school teachers. Guess your partner's favorite song, or both of you compile a list of your all-time favorite movies—and see if you have any in common. Take turns asking each other the names of the authors of classic books. See which one of you can name the most John Wayne movies or plays written by Shakespeare.

Games like these do more than help the two of you pass time. They also help you understand your partner better. You'll learn details you never knew about your wife's childhood or discover things you never dreamed she'd like.

Find a Sport You Both Enjoy

Enter an athletic club today, and you'll see women of all ages working out or doing aerobics. In the area of exercise, there is finally parity of the sexes. Today, women take part in as much regular physical activity as men do. Why not find an athletic activity that you and your wife can enjoy together?

A couple that can play doubles tennis with each other have an activity that they can share for most of a lifetime. And, if you find a sport that both of you enjoy a great deal, chances are good that you'll encourage each other to keep getting the exercise you need to stay healthy.

There are several sports you can participate in with your wife. You could play

golf or racquetball together. The two of
you could join a co-ed volleyball team or
play shuffleboard or horseshoes. If you
live near the water, you could sail. Just
remember that your goal is to get some
exercise and have fun with your wife. If
you're intensely competitive, reserve your
drive to win at all costs for the matches
played between you and your buddies. Any
sport you play with your wife should be
played for the purpose of having fun together—not proving that one of you can
triumph over the other.

Go Camping Together

Camping is one of the most romantic
activities a couple can share together. It
combines the splendid enjoyment of outdoors and nature with the cozy intimacy
that living in very close quarters brings.

Camping is not for everyone, of
course. If you have problems with mos-
quitoes, barking dogs, rain, hot, cold, no
lock on your door, bear mauling, intimacy,
or distance from a bathroom, camping
might not be for you. Don't rule it out,
however, until you have experienced it
alone with the woman you love. Breakfast
in bed at a luxury inn with antique furniture, coffee in the room, gift baskets, room
service, an indoor pool, and a hot tub

might sound more comfortable and conducive to intimacy than camping. You
must, however, take the plunge and nudge
your wife (and yourself) into the incredible experience of living in a tent together
at a secluded campground.

What makes this adventure so special
is that it turns both of your lives back to
a more innocent, youthful time. You feel
like two teen-agers on an overnight outing. Your senses of smell, touch, sound,
and sight are heightened by your surroundings—the sight of a chipmunk ven-
turing unusually close to your outdoor grill
in search of a crumb, the soft mist in the
air when you first emerge from your tent
in the morning, the symphony of ever-
changing bird calls, the powerful scent of
pine.

Simple activities are surprisingly fun,
such as searching for kindling wood and
knowing which kind works the best; walking together to the shower house at night,
carrying your flashlights, toothbrushes,
and soap dishes; enjoying salmon steak
and home fries prepared in your heavy
cast-iron frying pan over a wood fire you
built together; going for a swim in the
campground pond, surrounded by lush
greenery.

The joys of nature aside, the primary benefit of camping, though, is the romantic closeness that it fosters. The colder the tent at night, the closer you will snuggle together in your sleeping blanket. You eat together, swim together, and assemble and disassemble the tent together. You prepare your meals, clean up, and read together—and you hug a lot. You are far away from the daily routine of work and home. It is an incomparable time to focus on each other and the many blessings that God has bestowed upon your lives.

Chapter Twelve

Encourage Her Endeavors

In addition to striving to be the best mother, the best mate, and maybe the best second income earner, your wife might need something more in her life in order to feel personally fulfilled. She might work as a receptionist for a local dentist, but she might yearn to go back to school to become a social worker. She might manage a real estate office but long to take oil painting courses. She might be confined to the house with a newborn baby but still dream of going to law school. She might be a frustrated tennis player, or want to teach, take anthropology courses, or learn to roller-blade.

You should encourage your wife's search for growth and expansion out of the home. She will be a happier person and a better partner to live with if you do. I am saddened when I hear about a husband who insists upon his right to have a hot, freshly prepared meal ready for him on the table every day at 7:00 P.M., without flexibility. It is equally sad when a husband more or less forbids his wife to go out at night, whether to community meetings or shopping with friends, because he doesn't trust any baby sitters and he, the primary bread winner, wants to relax at night when he returns from work, not change diapers.

Weren't the slaves freed in the 1860s? In both cases, he is, in effect, shackling his wife's ankle to the radiator to limit her range of motion. There is nothing wrong with marrying a woman with the understanding that she will be in charge of running the house and taking care of the children. But, it is unfair and unrealistic for a husband to maintain complete control over his wife's schedule and prevent her from broadening herself as a person. There has to be some bending of the routine and sharing of the responsibilities to let her pursue endeavors that give her a greater sense of self-fulfillment.

A problem sometimes arises in this area because as a child the husband was brought up witnessing his mother prepare an elaborate supper for his work-exhausted father every day. If his own wife submits to the same kind of regimented lifestyle out of deference to him, her natural inclination to explore and expand her horizon will be repressed. And, sooner or later, her frustration will surface, whether or not either of them realizes the cause.

Taking the Initiative

Take time to evaluate how much time your wife has just for herself. Does she ever have the opportunity to pursue outside interests? If not, then it's up to you to see that she does. Encourage her interests and dreams because you love her dearly and you want her to be happy. Bring home adult education catalogs to see if anything attracts her eye. Help with baby-sitting arrangements. Take public transportation to work on the days that she has to drive from her job to her class or other activity. Surprise her on her birthday with a special gift such as a word processor or art supplies or a racquetball racquet, to show that you are totally behind her interests.

There are many benefits to you, as a husband, for your thoughtfulness and caring. First, and most important, your wife knows that her happiness is your highest priority. This, in turn, means that she will be a closer, more loving partner to you. Secondly, fringe benefits often result from the new skills that she develops as an adult. She might earn valuable income with her new training, whether it be in real estate, as a travel agent, a word processor operator, or she gains the skills necessary to open a new business from your home. If she goes to a professional school, the potential for new income is enormous.

Thirdly, having an outlet in new areas often makes for a calmer, more satisfied person. She will be a better mother, friend, and relative because of the confidence, pride, and increased self-worth that her new abilities produce. Lastly, she will become a much more interesting person to live with. She will share her new learning with you constantly, and you will become part of her new world. When you sit with each other at your weekly rendezvous, whispering loving words and sharing your recent experiences, she will tell you about the details of her new interest. She will talk about her teachers, her classmates, and her test results. You will relive the excitement with her. It will open your vistas to new ideas, new areas, new perspectives, and new worlds you never thought you'd ever be interested in. If both of you are having busy, interesting, full days, you will have much to share together (which is another reason why fixed weekly allotments of time spent alone between husband and wife are mandatory).

A long, successful marriage is attained by the growth of the partners as individuals—both of them—and the challenge and stimulation of the new interests that each of them brings to the union. So keep searching for activities that keep your relationship fresh and vibrant.

Take Courses Together

It can be great fun for a man and his wife to take courses together, whether they are totally recreational, like intermediate bridge, ballroom dancing, or silk screening, or more serious areas of study, such as religious seminars or a curriculum leading to a degree. Couples who went to high

school or college together are fortunate
to have already had this pleasure. But,
most couples never experienced school together, and it is a special treat for them to
sit together in a class. This experience
evokes the eagerness and innocence of
youth.

If you are both lucky enough to be
taking the same part-time program toward a degree, you can test each other.
You can also take notes for one another.
The two of you can drive to school together. You can even carry her books. Both
of you can wear matching sweaters and
pretend that you're two college freshman
walking hand-in-hand across the great
lawn of the campus. (Hopefully, you'll get
similar grades, so neither of you feels uneasy competing as classmates.)

It is also evidence of the great respect
you have for your wife if you take a course
together that your wife has chosen, but in
which you had no particular interest. By
going to her chosen classes, you are showing her that you are very interested in
what she has selected for herself. You are
also keeping her company (and insuring
that you are the one studying with her the
nights before an exam, not some hand-
some classmate!). If this curriculum is re-

ally a new adventure for her, then you are choosing to be part of her new world.

Attending classes is wonderfully stimulating to the mind and the spirit, and the exhilaration of being buoyed upward together is a special experience that you two can always look back on proudly in later years.

Two funny anecdotes come to mind when I recall the times that my wife and I attended class together. The first occurred on the first day of the first class we both attended as we began a long part-time course of study toward a degree in family counseling (yes, it was her selected specialty, and I came along for the ride). We had never done anything like this before, and here we were, the parents of four children, nervous and excited with anticipation. Both of us were decidedly self-conscious. Wanting to preserve our individuality, we chose to sit across from each other rather than next to each other (the chairs were all arranged in a circle rather than in rows facing the front of the room). We also decided to say that we were cousins rather than man and wife to avoid attracting too much attention to ourselves.

So, there we were, seated at our respective desks with our new empty notebooks and sharpened pencils, casually looking around, surveying the situation. Just as the teacher walked into the class, my eyes met my wife's eyes, and we both broke into the worst case of giggles either of us had ever experienced. At first there was a little bit of general noise going on around the room as people settled themselves into their seats, so our hysteria wasn't noticed. But, as things quieted down, our spasms became more noticeable. It was terrifying! There I was, knowing I was in deep trouble because I couldn't stop. I tried digging my nails into my skin, but it didn't help. Out of the corner of my eye, I saw my wife, likewise out of control, shaking in her seat. I finally got up and walked around a little bit, and my fit of giggles stopped, as did hers.

While the teacher gave his opening remarks, we both sat there, exhausted, wiping away our involuntary tears. (After this opening day fit of jitters, we settled down to work, sitting next to each other and acknowledging, when the subject came up, that we were indeed more closely related than cousins.) The years we spent studying and working together as a team were rich with discovery, one of the most special times of our entire marriage.

The other funny experience we had in class together occurred when my wife was in late pregnancy. Artistically inclined, she decided to take an evening ceramics course as part of an adult education program in a local high school. I had absolutely no interest in ceramics or pottery making or anything related to it, but I signed up to take the class with her, both to keep her company and to help her maneuver around in her uncomfortable physical condition.

The rest of the class, including my wife, seemed very serious about learning a new skill—molding the clay, working the wheel, painting the object, and preparing it for baking in the kiln. For my part, I could not share this seriousness and looked for ways to amuse myself during the two-hour sessions. I decided that to get the most out of the course and to help defray the hefty "materials fee" that they charged, I would make as many objects as I could turn out during the ten-session term.

While my classmates fine-tuned the shapes of the bowls and vases that each of them made during the ten weeks, I was turning out a whole menagerie of little animals, bridges, ladders, and fences. My little barnyard did not go unnoticed by the teacher or the other students, most of whom smiled politely at me as a curiosity, both for the audacious volume of my work and the fact that I was the only man in the class. My poor wife, less restrained than the others, found my creations hilarious. She spent most of the sessions laughing and chuckling to the point where she had trouble focusing on her own project. All in all, I acted like any other five-year-old with Play-Doh, but my wife and I have fond memories of our infamous ceramics class together. (As an addendum, she did finish a lovely bowl in the class, and most of my painted and glazed little doodads ended up in the bottom of our fish tank to amuse (?) the fish that scooted by.)

Listen to Her Dreams

Dreams about the future come up often during courtship, but have you taken the time lately to find out what your wife's current dreams are? She might dream of things she'd like to own, places she'd like to live in or visit, skills she'd like to acquire, a type of family she'd like to have, or accomplishments she'd like to achieve, either now or later on in life. Some of these longings are within easy grasp and realistic, while some are apparently beyond reach or are long shots at least.

Having special daydreams or goals and searching for them adds a wonderful dimension to the grind of our busy daily routines. Your spirits soar. Your thoughts are free. You can be anything or anywhere you wish. You are above the fetters of the work day. In your daydreams you are king, and you alone will determine your destiny (with the kind assistance of the Lord!).

Some daydreams, however, are more than a temporary respite; some are actually possible to achieve. It is these kinds of dreams that you can help your wife realize. Like a real estate agent who gets a commission on every sale, your reward is a share of the joy she feels on each of her successes. Use your energy, your ingenuity, your imagination, and your determination—whatever works—and go for it with her. If she wants to be in TV commercials, go with her to the library to get a book on the subject, help her pick out a photographer, work out a time when she can fit in some training courses on commercial acting, and help her go over her lines.

If she wants a little house in the country, with a pond and a horse and a couple of chickens, take a trip with her into nearby farm country. Go around with a broker looking at places that fit her description of a dream farm. Listen to her exclamations. You might find yourself falling in love with one of the houses as well. Even if you can't afford to buy it, you will have understood and shared one of her dreams.

If she always wanted to play the harp, privately look into the cost of lessons and surprise her on Mother's Day. Hand her (with a little love note) a gift certificate for ten beginner lessons at a local music school, then present your coup de grace. She opens the door of your study and there it stands, a magnificent harp, which you have rented on a trial basis from the school (after persuading them that this might lead to a long series of lessons). You have surprised your wife with something she always wanted, and your thoughtfulness in remembering her dream will mean as much, or more, to her than the gift itself.

Sharing and working on your dreams together is what makes a married lifetime together extraordinary. We all have the burden of surviving each day, during good times and bad times. We've all had a car that won't start one morning, precious children that wake up with a high fever, burglaries at our homes or businesses, furnaces that suddenly don't heat, and news that a close relative has suddenly passed away. We are able to stay above all this turmoil because of our faith in God, the loving relationships we have, and the magnificent dreams that we are forever aspiring to fulfill.

Chapter Thirteen

Keep the
Flame Burning

It seems routine today, and even fash-
ionable, for a man and his wife to be sepa-
rated overnight for days or weeks at a
time. Even the term *separate vacations*, a
development of the current generation,
sounds perfectly normal to some. Well,
this modern development can be detri-
mental to a healthy marriage. As it is, it
takes considerable planning and effort to
arrange for a husband and wife to get to
talk to each other, uninterrupted and
alone, in a routine busy week. (Isn't the
national average twenty-eight minutes per
week?) Unforeseen circumstances often

delay or prevent these precious moments of sharing. This creates a backlog of unexpressed communication. If that backlog is lengthy, it becomes almost impossible for two busy people to catch up. And, if the couple gives up and accepts the fact that they just won't be able to catch up, something is lost, forever, in their continuum of closeness. That is why a husband and wife must never be parted from one another for too long.

True, they are adults. They are independent individuals. They function perfectly well separately at work, at home, and at play. But, they are committed to being close friends as well as devoted partners, and separation drives a stake between them and moves them apart. In this context, planning a separate vacation or optional business trip seems like the willful creation of a rift. Sometimes a separation is unavoidable—a sudden business deal, an out-of-state funeral, an ill relative, an emergency at a vacation home. But, short of such an emergency, being apart, for longer than a night is a bad idea.

Men are created with powerful hormones that can get them into trouble. Even men who are blessed with the hap-

piest of marriages are vulnerable to temp-
tation. And their wives, even the most
faithful, are still living beings who are
subject to loneliness; they require com-
panionship and warmth. It is no secret
that Hollywood actors, whose work de-
mands frequent separation from their
families, do not boast the best marriages.
Unfortunately, the maxim "Out of sight,
out of mind" seems much closer to reality
than "Absence makes the heart grow
fonder."

A man determined to be a close husband should not select as his field of work
anything that obligates him to travel frequently on business trips. Men who are
often away might never hear a complaint
from their wives. Some wives are afraid to
complain about anything. Other wives
come to believe that the business trips are
necessary if they're going to have enough
money for their family's financial health.
Most times, probably, these women suffer
silently, troubled by loneliness during the
separations. They are just too proud to let
their mates, and certainly anyone else,
know about their inner pain. In the long
run, however, it is by far preferable for
husbands (and daddies) to resist the business trips (and the advancement and raises

that are often earned as a result) in order
to be home as much as possible, snuggling with their wives and children.

No Separate Vacations

Separate vacations are a cop-out and
a surrender. Instead of taking separate
vacations to bolster a marriage that is
failing, a couple should get good professional counseling and use a Caribbean trip
to work on some of their problems in a
romantic setting. If the impetus for separate holidays is an extreme conflict between the mates over what they enjoy doing on vacation (one likes to read all day,
one likes to shop; one is an early riser,
one loves the night life; one loves the
beach, and one hates sand), then let them
compromise. They can sleep in the same
room at night and spend the daytime
hours apart doing the things that each of
them likes but get together at preset times
during the day, such as meal times. This
will give them a chance to share with each
other what they did on their own and
serve as a reminder that they are, after
all, married to each other.

If two mates are leaning toward separate trips because of location (one likes
winter sports and one only likes warm

destinations), let them sit down, pretend they are adults, and work out a compromise. If they can agree on what they eat for supper every night and what movie they want to go to, then vacation destinations are relatively easy. Let them alternate by negotiation. "We'll go with your choice this year and mine next year." "If you take me to the Ritz Carlton, then I'll go—I mean I'll try to go—camping with you." In time, a couple will work out these problems, and like two old warriors, settle down to liking more of the same things.

Separate preferences are OK. Separate activities and tastes are OK. Separate bedrooms at night? Not OK. Minimize, or preferably eliminate, jobs or job titles that require regular company business trips. Avoid hobbies and avocations that separate you overnight. Do everything you can to keep your relationship firmly anchored by never straying too far from one another.

Come Up with Surprises

Just as predictability is very reassuring in relationships, unpredictability can be quite unsettling. On the other hand, too *much* predictability can become routine and boring. Periodic surprises, however, can be delightfully refreshing.

Surprises are fun. If chosen with care, they will charm your partner. She will feel that her man is always thinking of her, that he is fun, that he is full of life.

Every now and then, show up someplace where your wife least expects you. If you suddenly make an appearance at your son's third grade play (in which he has the role of a tree), you will thrill both your wife and your little boy. Most mothers routinely attend, but whenever a daddy shows up, it can be a unique treat.

Surprise her with gifts that she cannot believe you knew she wanted (maybe one of her close friends gave you a clue). Surprise her with gorgeous flowers on any and every occasion. Make your own bed one morning if that will astonish her. Have the kitchen table set when she gets home from work late one night and have some of her favorite dishes warming on the stove. Her expression, as well as her words, will show you how much she appreciates your efforts as she collapses in a chair while you serve her.

Unexpectedly hand her two tickets for a surprise trip that begins the next morning to mark a very important birthday of hers. (Most women prefer to celebrate special birthdays privately rather than with the speech-filled social occasions that men are accustomed to.) She will be flabbergasted at your bravado, then spend frantic hours on the phone making rapid-fire arrangements for house, children, job, and other obligations. "You are a crazy person," she probably will say with a big smile on her face, but you have shown her the extent to which you are willing to go to give this special day the lofty celebration it so rightfully deserves.

Try to recall the kinds of things you did for her before the two of you were married. In your heart, you are still dating her and still trying to impress and please her. It's a surefire way to keep your relationship vibrant.

Show Your Affection

It should become second nature to make physical contact with your wife whenever you are with her. I'm not referring to sexual touching, but rather touching as an expression of your fondness for her. Expressing your love in this way should go beyond the usual good-bye kiss in the morning and the welcoming hug in the evening. It is best done in private, but if it is done in public, it should be casual enough not to make anyone nearby uncomfortable. If you're both sitting next to each other listening to a speech at an organization dinner, lean on her gently. If you're walking together, hold hands or have her take your arm. In an elevator alone together (if you have at least two floors worth of time), pull her to you and give her a passionate hug. At a party at someone's house, when both of you happen to go into the host's kitchen for something at the same time, look both ways and then kiss her thoroughly and convincingly. Passing each other going through a narrow doorway? Don't waste the opportunity! It is pleasing and legal. Help her on and off with her coat. Take something heavy that she's carrying out of her hand. Showing your affection in this manner is comforting and always a reminder of your tenderness for each other.

Make Her Laugh

When Rockefeller was a baby, his father gave him blocks to play with—68th Street, 71st Street, 73rd Street, and 82d Street.

Sense of humor varies from person to person, and some people are naturally more gifted than others. Humor is a style, and a handy trait to develop. It can make life very interesting. It can also soften the impact of negative situations. When crises arise, you can help your mate keep things in perspective by pointing out the humor in the situation. (Hopefully, your wife also does this for you when the opportunity presents itself.)

If your wife is afraid that she doesn't have enough food for unexpected guests at her dinner party, offer to call in a bomb threat so that the house will have to be evacuated right before the main course. The humor is obviously corny, but it might remind her that there is a lighter side to life, and that these alleged catastrophes are not so serious after all. If you're standing in a long line or driving to an important appointment or stuck in a waiting room, make her laugh. Distract her, whenever possible, with humor when she seems unduly worried. Bring out her smile. After all, your ability to entertain her is probably one of the reasons she decided to marry you in the first place.

Daily Compliments

Compliments can be problematic. They are often embarrassing. Sometimes, they have a judgmental tone that makes the recipient feel as if he or she is being evaluated. "Your meat loaf is better than any meat loaf my old girlfriends made for me" or "Very good. You now know how to make a good crepe." Comments like these are in effect backhanded compliments, whether they're intended to be or not.

When compliments are sincerely given by an adoring husband, however, they tell his wife that she is truly appreciated. Loving compliments bring out her vitality, her sensuousness, and her inner joy.

Every day and every situation bring a new opportunity to compliment your wife. When you greet her in the evening after you return from work, you can ask her (after your affectionate hug and kiss), "How come you look so delicious?" And she, feeling wilted and exhausted after a long day, will suddenly come alive in response. When you see her without make-up first thing in the morning—when she would never allow another living soul to see her—tell her how gorgeous she is. When you gaze into her eyes, tell her she is stunning. Compliment her on her clothes and her hair, and don't forget those delicate shoulders. Tell her that you love how she feels.

Compliment her for the job she's doing as a mother—that your kids are so great because of the way she has raised them. Praise her for the lovely table she sets and the wondrous cooking she has prepared for the holiday meal.

After she has spent a long, tedious day doing spring cleaning, tell her that the house looks great, and although you married her just for her looks, you're impressed by what a great homemaker she's turned out to be. Compliment her on the special warmth in your household that she has created, and tell her what a pleasure it is to come home to that warmth.

Remember, voraciously eating a meal that she has prepared for you is definitely pleasing to your lady, but not a substitute for looking her in the eye and saying, "Thanks." Walking proudly into a wedding reception, with her arm resting on yours, indicates to her that you are proud to show her off in public. But, it is not as good as telling her directly, "You know, dear, you look gorgeous tonight." Having your secretary send her a bouquet of flowers on your anniversary is not the same as taking her hand and telling her tenderly,

"Marrying you is the best thing that ever happened to me."

The "thanks" and the compliments have to be clear and verbal. They also must be direct, not indirect or offhand. There must be endearing words used. If this is initially uncomfortable, do it little by little until it becomes totally natural. But, by all means let her hear this precious communication. It is important that she hear how much she means to you and how much you appreciate everything that she does for you.

Keep Refreshing Your Marriage

Aside from the constant work needed for the two of you to get along smoothly, there is a great challenge to prevent your relationship from growing stale. You both age, often at different rates and in different ways. What was new and exciting at certain times in your lives can become automatic and even a bore at later times.

It is important to continuously revitalize the most important relationship in your life—your marriage. There are no rules on how to do this. What is needed, really, is an awareness of the sanctity (and fragility) of this union. The methods used to keep a marriage fresh depend on the style and taste of the partners. The key word is *fresh*. Fresh ideas, new skills, new travel, new living locations, new relationships, new spiritual growth. All of these additions to your lives expand your horizons. They make you excited to wake up in the morning. They offer more tangible activities for a husband and wife to share together. New things stretch your abilities. They stretch your mind. They bring the excitement of challenge and the potential thrill of mastering untrodden areas.

Many couples have enjoyed going back to school, whether to learn how to ice a cake or how to become a travel agent. Many have attempted learning new sports or physical activities that they never would have considered when they were younger, such as wind surfing, parasailing, snowmobiling, board skiing, surfing, platform tennis, even flying a kite. Every time we are thrown into a new beginner's class, we become children again, and the tingly, nervous energy that is released rejuvenates us.

Unusual trips together, when they can be afforded, add new depth and breadth to our lives. Archeology digs and photo jungle safaris are great, as are rafting excursions and sailing between tropical islands. But, any trip to a new place has an element of adventure and mystery that makes a particular summer or winter a memorable one to recall.

Taking ballroom dancing lessons together can really be fun, and the new dance routines that you remember (one out of seven isn't too bad!) can be practiced at future dinners and celebrations. Perhaps you could produce and direct a play together in your local community center, or join a volunteer organization that assists relatives of hospitalized patients. Give time, as a couple, to a local geriatric center or a support group for recent émigrés.

You and your wife thus have brand-new areas to talk about, to think about, even to argue about. You are alive and humming as a couple. That calendar of advance plans is filling up rapidly. You two are getting so busy you begin to wonder how you're going to manage. You become alert to new ideas and begin listening when other people review what they are doing. You even have several innovative projects on the back burner. Suddenly, your marriage together seems fresh and full of fun (and all it took was a little imagination and the willingness to try something new).

Strive for Spiritual Advancement

Often, but not always, our wives are more advanced than we are spiritually. It is not a good practice to generalize, but women do have a gentle sensitivity and sometimes a greater ability to relate to God than their husbands do. Males seem to believe more in what they can touch or see, and the hormones and drives that they are born with often make spirituality much more difficult to achieve.

Given these generalities, a husband and wife are often at different places spiritually. If these different levels cause dissension between them, the situation can be very damaging. Religious practice and feeling is extremely personal and often fraught with guilt and resentment. A man and his wife have to decide on which religious service they will attend and how often. They must deal with the observance of holidays. They must decide on whether the children should go to a private school, and if so, which one. They must agree on where their charitable donations should go. They often have to discuss what religious activities their kids should partake in, and even which friends they should encourage or discourage.

Resolving these issues is really no different from dealing with other sensitive issues in marriage. A husband should respect and support his wife's spiritual level, and if she is striving to raise that level, he should support her just as he would in any of her other strivings. If he is indeed in conflict with her religious beliefs, he should be as tolerant as he would be with any other differences they have, even if they have to "agree to disagree" in the spiritual area. Deep down, though, if a man loves his woman and wants her to be content, he will work very hard to bridge the gap between them so that they can, hopefully, reach the same level of commitment in their daily lives to God. He should always treat any religious differences they have with respect and tolerance.

Perhaps more than in any other area of married life, this is an area of work that can bring you and your wife closer together. The key, though, is in loving each other very much and working hard on the eventual unity of your spiritual selves. The higher the spiritual level you attain together, the more meaningful and lofty your lives will be.

Chapter Fourteen

Final List of "Do's" and "Don'ts"

List of Do's

1. Do remind her every day that she is beautiful and young and sexy and desired and the one who inspires your insane, irrational love. ("Labeling" definitely works. If you tell her she is young and beautiful, she will feel and act young and beautiful.)

2. Look for every opportunity to help her in all of her activities and interests and physically assist her, as well, to conserve her strength.

3. Look for every chance to surprise her and treat her and bring her gifts. This

gives you a lifetime of ways to thrill the woman you adore.

4. Constantly add new ingredients to your lives together to keep your marriage fresh, vital, youthful, and interesting.

5. Schedule time alone together every week, away from children, work, and home, to share your feelings and souls—and make this time immovably fixed in stone.

6. Keep your intimate moments lofty and spiritual.

7. Seek out learning situations, physical activities, and hobbies that you can share together on an ongoing basis.

8. Give her the space and freedom to have her own pursuits and relationships and interests. Get to know everything about them.

9. She has the same right to spend your family's money as you do. Only joint financial accounts are allowed.

10. Play games together regularly, and fill her days with frivolity and humor.

11. Solicit and respect her opinions. She often has wiser and more sensitive insight than her husband.

12. Support and encourage her desire for spiritual advancement.

13. Find out what her dreams are and spend a lifetime trying to fulfill them for her.

14. Savor each day and treat it as a precious gift.

List of Don'ts

1. Don't separate for even one night unless it is absolutely necessary. The phrase "I have no choice" is always questionable.

2. Don't say anything negative about her publicly, even if at that moment you absolutely detest her. She is the romantic attachment of your life and the reason for your being.

3. Don't neglect or downgrade anything important to her, including relatives, ideas, dreams, work, friends, and hobbies. What is hers is yours.

4. Don't let one day pass without giving her physical affection, an expression of gratitude, and some communication of a complimentary nature.

5. Don't let one day pass without knowing everything she did that day—to whom she spoke and about what she is feeling and thinking.

6. Don't ever, *ever* deliberately cause her physical or mental pain.

7. Don't take her for granted. She is a miracle with which you have been blessed.

More Good

Books from

Vital Issues Press...

We welcome comments from our readers. Feel free to write to us at the following address:

Editorial Department
Vital Issues Press
P.O. Box 53788
Lafayette, LA 70505

Legacy Builders
Dad, What Does Your Life
Say to Your Wife and Children?
by Jim Burton

Today, feminism and changing economics make it difficult for men to understand their role in a society that seems to devalue their inherent qualities. Discover how men can build a legacy— and why America so desperately needs men to understand their role in the family and society.

ISBN 1-56384-117-7

ADD:
. . . the facts . . . the fables
. . . hope for your family
by Theresa Lamson

ADD (Attention Deficit Disorder) is often ridiculed by those cynics who deny its existence and by those who dogmatically insist that "spanking your child more" would correct all of his behavior problems. However, if you're the parent of a child who suffers this disorder, you are painfully aware that ADD is real. Cheer up! You're not a bad parent. You need hope, encouragement, and biblical solutions—this book offers you all three. In addition, the author shares valuable knowledge from the secular pool of current information.

ISBN 1-56384-121-5

The Basic Steps to Successful Homeschooling
by Vicki A. Brady

If you are a parent already convinced of the moral and intellectual benefits of home education, this book is for you. Working on the premise that home education is a wise decision, Vicki Brady, an expert in the field, provides the reader with a practical, nuts-and-bolts approach to implementing a system of home education. Because of its clear, step-by-step format, this book serves as an invaluable guide for beginner and expert alike in the field of home education. The decision to homeschool is a serious, often intimidating one, but one that serves many families well, if carried out properly. This book will make the decision less daunting, providing home educators with a wealth of knowledge and, therefore, confidence.

ISBN 1-56384-113-4

Anyone Can Homeschool: How to Find What Works for You
by Terry Dorian, Ph.D., and Zan Peters Tyler

Honest, practical, and inspirational, *Anyone Can Homeschool* assesses the latest in homeschool curricula and confirms that there are social as well as academic advantages to home education. Both veteran and novice homeschoolers will gain insight and up-to-date information from this important new book.

ISBN 1-56384-095-2

Do Angels Really Exist?
Separating Fact from Fantasy
by Dr. David O. Dykes

Have you ever seen an angel? Don't be too quick to answer "no." For most of us, angels evoke images of winged, white figures frolicking from one cloud to another. But, according to the Bible, angels are God's armored warriors ready to protect His kingdom in heaven, as well as His beloved followers on earth. By citing dozens of fascinating angel encounters, the author presents evidence that angels roam the earth today, protecting and comforting God's people. You might be encountering angels without even knowing it.

ISBN 1-56384-105-3

The Gender Agenda:
Redefining Equality
by Dale O'Leary

All women have the right to choose motherhood as their primary vocation. Unfortunately, the radical feminists' movement poses a threat to this right—the right of women to be women. In *The Gender Agenda,* author Dale O'Leary takes a spirited look at the feminist movement, its influence on legislation, and its subsequent threat to the ideals of family, marriage, and motherhood. By shedding light on the destructiveness of the radical feminists' world view, O'Leary exposes the true agenda of the feminist movement.

ISBN 1-56384-122-3

The First Lady:
A Comprehensive View of
Hillary Rodham Clinton
by Peter & Timothy Flaherty

Is Hillary Rodham Clinton a modern career woman or an out-of-control feminist? In this compelling account of her life, the authors suggest that Mrs. Clinton has been misrepresented in the media and misunderstood by both conservatives and liberals alike.

ISBN 1-56384-119-3

Freud's War with God:
Psychoanalysis vs. Religion
by Dr. Jack Wright, Jr.

Freud's hostility to religion was an obsession: he dismissed all religious belief as a form of mental illness—a universal neurosis—and devoted his life's work to attacking it in whatever form it might appear. No other single theorist has had the impact on psychiatrists, psychologists, and social workers as has Sigmund Freud. Dr. Jack Wright demonstrates how his influence can be felt in such varied phenomena as gay rights, outcome-based education, and the false memory syndrome—all elements of the culture war that rebel against God and religious orthodoxy.

ISBN 1-56384-067-7

Health Begins in Him:
Biblical Steps to Optimal
Health and Nutrition
by Terry Dorian, Ph.D.

This book is offered as a resource for all those seeking knowledge about how to change their lives in ways that will enable them to preserve and maintain optimal health. Health and nutrition aficionados will also find this volume essential, thanks to the guidelines, scientific studies, and testimonials. Clear, concise, and lively dialogue makes this a very readable directory on foods, food preparation, lifestyle changes, and suggestions for renewal. Terry Dorian, Ph.D. has been a whole-foods advocate for more than twenty years and conducts seminars that teach degenerative disease prevention and cures.

ISBN 1-56384-081-2

From Earthquakes to Global Unity:
The End Times Have Begun
by Paul McGuire

From the controversial GATT treaty to the move toward a cashless society, we are witnessing events that have the capacity to alter our world significantly—and irrevocably. McGuire's fascinating research reveals how some of these changes might soon affect us all.

ISBN 1-56384-107-X

Conservative, American & Jewish— I Wouldn't Have It Any Other Way

by Jacob Neusner

Neusner has fought on the front lines of the culture war and here writes reports about sectors of the battles. He has taken a consistent, conservative position in working with federal agencies involved with the humanities and the arts and in his work as a distinguished research professor of religious studies. Engaging, persuasive, controversial in the best sense, these essays set out to change minds and end up touching the hearts and souls of their readers.

ISBN 1-56384-048-0

A Jewish Conservative Looks at Pagan America

by Don Feder

If you like political commentary but not the dry prose in which it's often written, you will be delighted with the writing of Don Feder. With unparalleled eloquence, he defines faith, family, and morality in the same terms as most hardworking Americans. Feder's gift as wordsmith is showcased most compellingly in this package of his best columns, addressing abortion, gay rights, a Christian America, multiculturalism, foreign policy, and more.

ISBN 1-56384-036-7 Trade Paper
ISBN 1-56384-037-5 Hardcover

I Shot an Elephant in My Pajamas—
The Morrie Ryskind Story

by Morrie Ryskind with John H. M. Roberts

The Morrie Ryskind story is a classic American success story. The son of Russian Jewish immigrants, Ryskind went on to attend Columbia University and achieve legendary fame on Broadway and in Hollywood, win the Pulitzer Prize, and become a noted nationally syndicated columnist. From his successful collaborations with such Broadway legends as George and Ira Gershwin to his work with the Marx Brothers, Ryskind's career was a remarkable one. This lively chronicle of his life is as entertaining as it is moving.

ISBN 1-56384-000-6

The Truth about False Memory Syndrome

by James G. Friesen, Ph.D.

With his new book on false memory syndrome, Dr. Jim Friesen cuts through all the misinformation being bandied about on this subject. Through harrowing, yet fascinating, case studies, dealing with everything from sexual to Satanic ritual abuse, Friesen educates the reader on the most complex coping mechanism of the human psyche. A pioneer in the treatment of multiple personality disorder, Friesen dispels the myths surrounding FMS and victims of abuse as no tabloid or talk show can.

ISBN 1-56384-111-8

Getting Out:
An Escape Manual for Abused Women
by Kathy L. Cawthon

Four million women are physically assaulted by their husbands, ex-husbands, and boyfriends each year. Of these millions of women, nearly 4,000 die. Kathy Cawthon, herself a former victim of abuse, uses her own experience and the expertise of law enforcement personnel to guide the reader through the process of escaping an abusive relationship. *Getting Out* also shows readers how they can become whole and healthy individuals instead of victims, giving them hope for a better life in the future.

ISBN 1-56384-093-6

Outcome-Based Education:
The State's Assault
on Our Children's Values
by Peg Luksik & Pamela Hobbs Hoffecker

From the enforcement of tolerance to the eradication of moral absolutes, Goals 2000 enjoins a vast array of bureaucratic entities under the seemly innocuous umbrella of education. Unfortunately, traditional education is nowhere to be found in this controversial, strings-attached program. In this articulate and thoroughly documented work, Luksik and Hoffecker reveal the tactics of those in the modern educational system who are attempting to police the thoughts of our children.

ISBN 1-56384-025-1

Out of Control—
Who's Watching Our Child
Protection Agencies?
by Brenda Scott

This book of horror stories is true. The deplorable and unauthorized might of Child Protection Services is capable of reaching into and destroying any home in America. No matter how innocent and happy your family may be, you are one accusation away from disaster. Social workers are allowed to violate constitutional rights and often become judge, jury, and executioner. Every year, it is estimated that over 1 million people are falsely accused of child abuse in this country. You could be next, says author and speaker Brenda Scott.

ISBN 1-56384-080-4

Children No More:
How We Lost a Generation
by Brenda Scott

Child abuse, school yard crime, gangland murders, popular lyrics laced with death motifs, twisted couplings posing as love on MTV and daytime soap operas (both accessible by latchkey children), loving parents portrayed as the enemy, condom pushers, drug apologists, philandering leaders . . . is it any wonder that heroes and role models are passé? The author grieves the loss of a generation but savors a hope that the next can be saved.

ISBN 1-56384-083-9

Journey into Darkness: Nowhere to Land
by Stephen L. Arrington

This story begins on Hawaii's glistening sands and ends in the mysterious deep with the Great White shark. In between, the author finds himself trapped in the drug smuggling trade—unwittingly becoming the "Fall Guy" in the highly publicized John Z. DeLorean drug case. The author recounts his horrifying prison experience and allows the reader to take a peek at the source of hope and courage that helped him survive.

ISBN 1-56384-003-3

High on Adventure: Stories of Good, Clean, Spine-tingling Fun
by Stephen L. Arrington

In the first volume of this exciting series of adventure stories, you'll meet a seventeen-and-a-half-foot Great White shark face-to-face, dive from an airplane toward the earth's surface at 140 M.P.H., and explore a sunken battle cruiser from World War II in the dark depths of the South Pacific Ocean. Author and adventurer Stephen Arrington tells many exciting tales from his life as a navy frogman and chief diver for The Cousteau Society, lacing each story with his Christian belief and outlook that life is an adventure waiting to be had.

ISBN 1-56384-082-0

High on Adventure II:
Dreams Becoming Reality
by Stephen L. Arrington

Join the former Cousteau diver again as he travels around the world, revisiting old acquaintances from the deep and participating in dangerous, new adventures. In this exciting second volume of the series, Arrington even explores the underwater lava flow of an active volcano—while it is in progress!

ISBN 1-56384-115-0

The Best of HUMAN EVENTS:
Fifty Years of Conservative
Thought and Action
Edited by James C. Roberts

Before Ronald Reagan, before Barry Goldwater, since the closing days of World War II, HUMAN EVENTS stood against the prevailing winds of the liberal political Zeitgeist. HUMAN EVENTS has published the best of three generations of conservative writers—academics, journalists, philosophers, politicians: Frank Chodorov and Richard Weaver, Henry Hazlitt and Hans Sennholz, William F. Buckley and M. Stanton Evans, Jack Kemp and Dan Quayle. A representative sample of their work, marking fifty years of American political and social history, is here collected in a single volume.

ISBN 1-56384-018-9

Notes

Notizen